HOW FIRM A FOUNDATION:
VOICES OF THE EARLY LITURGICAL MOVEMENT

*Compiled and
introduced by
Kathleen Hughes, RSCJ*

D0054483

 LITURGY
TRAINING
PUBLICATIONS

CONTENTS

ACKNOWLEDGMENTS

This book collects materials from numerous sources. We are grateful to their publishers. Specific acknowledgments are in the endnotes.

Copyright © 1990, Archdiocese of Chicago. All rights reserved.
Liturgy Training Publications
1800 North Hermitage Avenue
Chicago IL 60622-1101
1-800-933-1800

Printed in the United States of America.

Edited by Elizabeth Hoffman
Design by Jane Kremsreiter
Cover design by Carolyn Riege
Cover art from *The Catholic Art Quarterly* 6, no. 1 (1942): 27. Mary Katherine Finnegan

1 Introduction
14 Karl Adam
20 Donald Attwater
23 Lambert Beauduin
29 Florence Berger
32 Ade Bethune
38 Bernard Botte
44 Pascal Botz
49 Louis Bouyer
53 William Busch
57 Paul Bussard
60 Daniel Cantwell
64 John Carroll
66 Thomas Carroll
69 Odo Casel
72 Dorothy Coddington
75 Patrick Cummins
78 Dorothy Day
83 Catherine de Hueck Doherty
86 Alcuin Deutsch
90 Godfrey Diekmann
100 Gregory Dix
103 Michael Ducey
106 Benedict Ehmann

109	Gerald Ellard	201	John P. O'Connell
113	Romano Guardini	203	Pius Parsch
120	Paul Hallinan	206	Hans Ansgar Reinhold
124	Martin B. Hellriegel	214	John Ross-Duggan
128	Ildefons Herwegen	217	Leo Rudloff
131	Reynold Hillenbrand	219	Mary Perkins Ryan
136	Cecilia Himebaugh	221	Shawn Sheehan
138	Johannes Hofinger	225	Gerard Sloyan
143	Clifford Howell	231	Joseph F. Stedman
146	William Huelsmann	234	Basil Stegman
149	Placid Jordan	236	Georgia Stevens
151	Josef A. Jungmann	239	Anselm Stolz
160	James Kleist	241	Samuel Stritch
163	Bernard Laukemper	243	Kathryn Sullivan
166	Maurice Lavanoux	247	Columban Thuis
169	William Leonard	249	Gerald Vann
172	Frederick McManus	251	Ermin Vitry
177	Columba Marmion	254	Justine Ward
179	Michael Mathis	257	Aloysius Wilmes
181	Thomas Merton	259	Mary Fabyan Windeatt
186	Virgil Michel	261	Damasus Winzen
190	Josephine Morgan	265	John D. Wright
192	Joseph P. Morrison	270	Notes
195	Therese Mueller	281	Notes on Illustrations
198	Jane Marie Murray	284	Index

INTRODUCTION

One of the great pleasures of life is to introduce friends who don't yet know each other, to watch with delight as they become acquaintances, take up the conversation, find a mutually enriching topic, and then become so engrossed in one another that they barely miss you as you slip away. That is the pleasure awaiting me as you pick up this book, for the persons I am quoting have become my friends and I am eager for others to get to know them.

It all started when I decided to write the biography of Godfrey Diekmann, a work still in progress. Through reading and through interviews with Godfrey and numerous other men and women, veterans of the "liturgical apostolate" as they called it, an intriguing picture began to form in my mind's eye of the early liturgical movement in the United States and of the personalities of the "movers." I found it fascinating to recognize the genesis of some of the reforms of Vatican Council II in the vision of Virgil Michel and his collaborators, the annual conferences of the National Liturgical Weeks, the articles in *Orate Fratres, America, Commonweal* and other journals.

The liturgical movement, at the beginning only an abstraction for me, soon became a collection of faces—a group of people who had hopes and dreams for the celebration of a fully renewed liturgy. In these pages I present to you a group of people who were every bit as human as you and I, whose ideas were sometimes brilliant but not always right, who forged the connection between worship and the marketplace yet occasionally lapsed into monastic romanticism, who suffered the same frustrations as we do at the slowness of change. And slow it was, especially in the beginning. William Busch, one of the pioneers, once lamented: "Interest had to be aroused, apathy to be overcome, and there was misunderstanding and no small amount of opposition."

The pioneers faced an uphill battle. Modernism was still stalking the theological community at the beginning of this century. Those who promoted the doctrine of the Mystical Body, the doctrine upon which a new ecclesiology and consequent liturgical renewal was based, were highly suspect. Their orthodoxy was doubted and sometimes attacked. The pioneers were *on* fire, but also *under* fire. According to one account of the early heroic days of the movement:

> There was terrible confusion everywhere. If somebody did not like a devotion or prayer, he simply called it "unliturgical." Others, on the contrary, used the word liturgical for name-calling. A person who was just odd or "arty" or somehow different in his views was given the stamp: He is a liturgist. You could hardly say anything worse of him under the law of Christian charity. Being liturgical smacked not only of heresy, stubbornness and a hankering for novelty, it was almost a moral blemish. (*Orate Fratres* 13 [1939], 152)

It should be no surprise, therefore, that in their speaking and writing, the pioneers quote the popes rather more frequently than might be our inclination today. They discovered in papal pronouncements, particularly in the writings of Pius X,

Pius XI, and Pius XII, vindication for their theology as well as overt support for what came to be known as "the Cause," the goal which bound them together: that the liturgy and, strictly speaking the eucharist, becomes the vitalizing and directing principle of the Christian life.

As their brief biographies will demonstrate, our liturgical ancestors were people of many different gifts, personalities and insights. In the early days of the liturgical movement every skill was joined—that of the writer, the theologian, the historian, the social activist, the elder statesperson, the homemaker, the artist, the musician, even the philanthropist. Most wandered into liturgy by the back door, through scripture, systematics, patristics or history, for example, or as writers and translators.

For some, the liturgy became their love because they simply happened to be in the right place at the right time. Such was true of the artist Ade Bethune. Ade was living at the Catholic Worker house with Dorothy Day when Daniel Lord offered Dorothy one scholarship to the Summer School of Catholic Action. Ade was invited to take advantage of the scholarship and thus met Gerald Ellard who was teaching liturgy that summer. From that point on Ade's study of liturgy profoundly influenced her artistic expression.

Godfrey Diekmann, too, was in the right place at the right time. He was a young monk, recently returned to St. John's from his studies at Sant' Anselmo, when he was appointed to assist Virgil Michel in the publication of *Orate Fratres*. At Virgil's sudden death in 1938, Godfrey was named the editor of the magazine.

Most of the pioneers were self-taught in the field of liturgy. Perhaps that accounts for some of the becoming modesty among them as well as the respect, the esteem and the obvious affection they had for one another. Such affection is evident in the *Proceedings* of the National Liturgical Weeks as they introduced their colleagues with praise and warmth. It is evident, too, in their obituaries, filled with glowing tributes from their friends: "the theologian of the liturgy"; "the liturgist without peer"; "an excellent and genial host"; "a gentle scholar"; "a man of practical understanding as well as deep piety"; "with him there was no credibility gap"; "her humility before God was an inspiration"; "no one who heard him could remain untouched by the fire of his faith"; "just to hear her name made you feel good all over."

In the beginning the number of pioneers was small. Many knew each other; many collaborated on a regular basis. They met in each other's homes or rectories to plan the next conference or brainstorm an attractive summer school program. They kept in touch by letters; they visited one another in times of sickness; they preached at each other's anniversaries and funerals. For years there was only a shoestring budget to support their work and often they gave their services without remuneration. Some endeavors, such as the publication of the magazine *Liturgy and Sociology,* were short-lived for lack of funding. Other initiatives, for example, the founding of the Pius X School of Liturgical Music, relied on the generosity of a major donor.

In the course of my reading and interviews certain names began to stand out. I cannot pretend that the collection of personalities I have assembled is exhaustive. It is, in fact, more quixotic than inclusive. A word about my choices may help. A number of the early American leaders had studied in Europe under the tutelage of scholars like Karl Adam, Lambert Beauduin, Anselm Stolz, Odo Casel and Ildefons Herwegen. They returned to the United States on fire with a vision of church and worship which they began to communicate to others through the printed word of *Orate Fratres,* founded in 1926; through the publications of St. John's Popular Liturgical Library; and through conferences which began modestly in various cities as day-long events and, by 1940 under the sponsorship of the Benedictine Liturgical Conference, became national gatherings. Some Europeans are included in this collection, either because they had educated Americans or because, like Columba Marmion, they had been read and had profoundly influenced so many in the field.

A number of Benedictine abbots are included: Alcuin Deutsch of St. John's Abbey, Collegeville; Columban Thuis of St. Joseph's Abbey, Louisiana; Damasus Winzen of Mount Savior, New York; Leo Rudloff of Dormition Abbey in Jerusalem and Weston Priory in Vermont; Patrick Cummins of Conception Abbey, Missouri. We need to acknowledge the support which Benedictines lent to the liturgical movement in the early days, in educating their members, in sponsoring publications and conferences, and in serving as oases of good liturgical development.

Similarly, several bishops are included in this collection. Perhaps most surprising will be the presence of Bishop John Carroll of Baltimore, a man who antedated the liturgical movement, but who had the wisdom 200 years ago to speak in favor of the vernacular as a necessary liturgical innovation if the church was to find a home on these shores. Were Carroll alive today he might be a prominent spokesperson for serious liturgical inculturation.

Other bishops were more recent supporters of the liturgical movement: Samuel Stritch, a gregarious and well-loved leader of the church of Chicago, was the patron of the first Liturgical Week in the United States and preached to those who had assembled for this historic event in the Holy Name Cathedral.

Bishop John Wright was an enthusiastic promoter of the liturgical conferences and a speaker at several. His classic homily on the Emmaus story, *"Sperabamus,"* delivered at the National Liturgical Week of 1960, may still serve to reinvigorate all latter-day disciples who believe their hopes shattered.

Another bishop included in these pages is Paul Hallinan who, to his great amazement at finding himself appointed to the Liturgical Preparatory Commission of Vatican II, declared that he was "surprised, delighted and scared." With the untiring assistance of Frederick R. McManus, American *peritus* on the Commission, Hallinan schooled himself in matters liturgical and became an enthusiastic promoter of liturgical reform until his death in 1968.

Not included but deserving of affectionate mention are the many other bishops who assisted in the United States liturgical apostolate, especially Cardinal John Dearden of Detroit, Bishop Vincent Waters of Raleigh, Archbishop Edwin O'Hara of Great Falls and Kansas City, Archbishop Karl Alter of Cincinnati and Bishop Charles Buswell of Pueblo.

For the rest of this collection, I relied on the proceedings of National Liturgical Weeks, as well as on essays, homilies, letters, speeches, biographies, histories, obituaries, personal notes, and on the reminiscences of Godfrey Diekmann and others to single out men and women who had played a prominent role in the liturgical movement *prior* to the Council. (A second volume has already been begun in order to recognize those tireless scholars and pastors, most of whom are with us to this day, who took up "the Cause" after Vatican II.) Each person, in turn, led me to others, and the circle of friends I was forming continued to grow.

As I came to know these people, I noticed some interesting patterns. These liturgists not only *lived* the liturgy but a remarkable number *died* liturgically: foremost among them, of course, would be Odo Casel who died after singing the Preface of the Exsultet at the Easter Vigil. Virgil Michel died on the last day of the liturgical year, as did Dorothy Day. William Huelsmann, an outstanding pastor, died on Good Shepherd Sunday. Abbot Patrick Cummins, a great believer in people, died on St. Valentine's Day. Lambert Beauduin died at the beginning of the octave of church unity, a cause dear to his heart.

Quite possibly liturgical hagiography may be responsible for other edifying deaths: It is said, for example, that John P. O'Connell died as he said, "Maranatha. Come, Lord Jesus."

Michael Mathis, on his deathbed, is reported to have remarked, "My Amen is all I have left."

The words of the liturgy may well have been on the lips of many of the pioneers. Reading through this collection, you will be struck by the manner in which the liturgical texts are so easily cited in speech and writing. It appears to be taken for granted that one's audience is literate in Latin and in the full reference when, for example, an Introit *incipit* is used.

It is equally clear that liturgical literacy is due in large measure to the use of hand missals which, for the first time, allowed people to "pray the Mass," rather than pray at Mass. While liturgists today might decry the use of missal-ettes, and with good reason, a nod of thanks is appropriate to all who labored to put the texts of the Mass into the hands of the assembly. The astonishing success of hand missals prepared by Stedman, Bussard and others is one index of the desire of the people of God for more active participation in the worship of the church.

While touching on language, let me say a word about some difficult editorial choices. The pioneers were remarkably sensitive to issues of justice and it is on that basis that I altered their words to be inclusive of men and women; exclusive language would have been a needless obstacle to appreciating the thoughts of these men and women. Where possible and for a similar reason, language referring to God was also modified. On the other hand, I decided *not* to remove terms no longer in use or in vogue. The Holy Ghost remains a ghost; the canon does not become a eucharistic prayer; references to days and customs no longer observed are here retained, such as rogation and ember days. The meaning of these days of spiritual renewal, fasting and inter-cession is clear from the context. Their inclusion may also serve to stir up the curiosity of post–Vatican II students of the liturgy.

Perhaps occasionally more jarring in this collection is a theological vocabulary which has been, to a large extent, superseded by the theology of Vatican II. I refer, for example, to the language of "souls" rather than human persons, to "applying the merits" of the "sacrifice" of the Mass and the "fruits" of the Mass. Every age has its own unique theological vocabulary. It seems important to retain such terms as part of a larger vision of "living the liturgy," a topic ubiquitous in these pages. The role of the laity, the priesthood of believers, the role of the parish, the unfolding of the liturgical year, the texts of the Mass as prayer, the relationship of Sunday and the rest of the week—all of these form some of the preoccupations of our pioneers as they try to articulate the meaning of living the liturgy.

What were the fundamental concerns that preoccupied the pioneers and that bound these men and women together, though so different in gifts and in temperament? Three concerns seem paramount: the theology of the Mystical Body of Christ, head and members; active participation in the worship of the one body; the relationship of liturgy and life. Clearly, the liturgical movement, and the preoccupations of its adherents, did not develop in a vacuum, but resulted because of the convergence of several great movements of the early 20th century.

It was the biblical movement that developed and expounded the Pauline doctrine of the Mystical Body of Christ. Imagine the extraordinary shift from an earlier ecclesiology of the church as the perfect society to the church as the body of Christ. If the church is the perfect society, then only the perfect might participate in its worship—and a sense of unworthiness and the appropriateness of ritual exclusion by architecture, language and arcane rites were consequences largely unchallenged. But then we awakened to the Pauline image of the body of Christ and this development implied another way to worship. This new understanding of the nature of the church and of worship was communicated, above all, not in talking about liturgy but in the very doing of it. Visualize, if you will, the first dialogue Mass and its effect on persons accustomed only to praying *at Mass,* not praying *the Mass!* One participant in such a Mass celebrated in 1930 described its impact as that of the church coming alive, with all members as co-offerers, all as co-responsible because of the basic reality of baptism. It became clear that all gathered around the altar are equal and all are doing the most important work the church can do.

These biblically founded insights developed quite naturally into the liturgical movement strictly speaking. The energies of the pioneers converged in a single direction—that of active participation, a phrase which became the movement's rallying cry, although this phrase did not always have a univocal meaning for those who were using it. In light of the doctrine of the Mystical Body, active participation had to do with the sincerity of one's Amens. It had to do with self-offering. It had to do with joining oneself to the sacrifice of the one and only leader of prayer, Jesus Christ. The corollary of the theology of the Mystical Body is that all gathered at the table are co-offerers with Christ and all must struggle with the demands which "Amen" makes.

So, active participation became the goal of the liturgical movement, a goal to be achieved by numerous means: more imaginative observances of feasts and seasons and their special rites, care for environment, congregational singing, dialogue Masses, participation in processions, use of the Stedman you-can't-get-lost Missal or the leaflet Missal or other worship aids. Above all, the use of the vernacular became a symbol of the desire for full, conscious and active participation. The vernacular was championed more or less aggressively depending on circumstances—sometimes it was even explicitly proscribed, as at the Assisi Conference of 1956. The story is told that one of the speakers broke the silence and addressed the question of the vernacular. By the next morning a Vatican representative had returned to Rome. There was a good deal of anxiety about this turn of events until it was discovered that the man had fled Assisi not because the "v" word had been spoken but because his bed was infested with fleas.

The third of the interrelated movements at the turn of the century was the social movement—or in contemporary terms, the movement for peace and justice. At the liturgy we commit ourselves to active participation in the work of constructing the kingdom with Christ—what Virgil Michel called the work of social regeneration. Our contemporary discussion of the relationship between liturgy and social justice would have been inconceivable to most of the pioneers. There was no question that liturgy and justice were essential to each other.

For Virgil Michel, to take one example, the racial question, justice with regard to the distribution of the land, the crusade to establish a Christian social order and the movement for Christian reunion were the most logical and consistent concerns of one who entered into the sacrifice of Christ. You will find in these pages a remarkable breadth of interest and social concern: Moslem-Jewish relations; the work of the missions; ecumenism; labor unions, housing committees, and the provision of medical care for the poor; the campaign for racial equality. According to the pioneers, these are among the issues that one schooled in the liturgy must take to heart.

Our liturgical ancestors clearly recognized that the way one lived one's life was a litmus test of the authenticity of one's worship. They knew in their bones that, in light of the inseparable nature of liturgy and life, one must worship the same God on Sunday and during the week, one must recognize that the equality we know at the table of the Lord must be celebrated at all our other tables; one must understand, perhaps daily more deeply, the demands accepted with every liturgical Amen. This is what was on the minds and in the hearts of the pioneers. Justice was part and parcel of the early liturgical movement. The pioneers worked tirelessly for active participation in worship, not because they liked to play church but because they were convinced that it would lead to a new social order. This theme is more pervasive than any other in the pages that follow. Some of the quotations are remarkably contemporary; much of the vision of the pioneers is yet to be realized.

Assembling this collection happens to coincide with several significant anniversaries. The *Constitution on the Sacred Liturgy* of the Second Vatican Council was promulgated just over 25 years ago. The definitive vote on the Constitution took place 60 years to the day after Pius x's famous *motu proprio,* "On the Restoration of Sacred Music," urged active and intelligent participation in the liturgy. The year 1990 marks the 50th anniversary of the first National Liturgical Week in the United States; 1991 will mark the 65th anniversary of the publication of *Orate Fratres/Worship,* an event to which many would point as the genesis of the liturgical movement in North America. Each of these anniversaries invites us to gratitude for the extraordinary progress of liturgical reform in our own day and to renewed dedication to the work of liturgical renewal.

As I assembled these texts, I became convinced of their present day usefulness, convinced of the necessity of understanding who these people were, what they read, what motivated their work, what vision they lived by—precisely in order to understand the reforms of Vatican II and, now that the externals are in place, to return to the essentials in a fresh way. It is Frederick McManus who convinced me of the importance of returning to these sources. In an address to the National Liturgical Week of 1961 McManus anticipated the need to achieve a deep understanding of all that would issue from the Council, and he proposed that the pioneers could serve as our guides. Speaking in tribute of Gerald Ellard, McManus said:

> Father Ellard and others like him are our present and, we pray, future source of understanding of the holy liturgy.

When the documents of the papal liturgical revival appear, it is possible for the commentators and interpreters to study them in a vacuum—as if they had no history or background—which is poor liturgical science and still poorer canon law; it is possible to examine them soundly and scientifically, with reason and prudence—which is good; and it is above all possible to seek and to find the real meaning of these changes and developments simply from the teaching and preaching of people like Father Ellard—and to name only two others happily with us, Monsignor Hellriegel and Father Reinhold. They know why it is all happening and in all humility we must be willing to go to them for the inner sense of liturgical development.

For a variety of reasons the liturgical movement has gotten bogged down. The fire of the founders is rarely visible among us. There is a good deal of discouragement. Some say that the liturgical movement actually ended at Vatican II. Others say the liturgical movement realized all of its goals when the post-Conciliar Consilium and the International Commission on English in the Liturgy produced a new library of liturgical books. What is clear is that the liturgical movement became institutionalized and that it needs to recover its prophetic character. Who better than the pioneers to reenergize our efforts by rooting us once again in their vision that the liturgy become the heart and center of the Christian life?

Many people helped me in this work. The following graciously responded to letters and phone calls for help: Hugh Baumann, OSB, St. Joseph Abbey, St. Benedict, Louisiana; Dr. Alfred Berger, Hilton Head, North Carolina; Mary Berchmans, APB, Brooklyn, New York; Catherine Carroll, RSCJ, Albany, New York; Christian Ceplecha, OSB, archivist at Illinois Benedictine College, Lisle, Illinois; Father Charles Gusmer, Immaculate Conception Seminary, South Orange, New Jersey; Vivian Ivantic, OSB, archivist at St. Scholastica Priory, Chicago; Cindy Klazura, *The New World*, Chicago; Mary Louise Padberg, RSCJ, archivist of the Religious of the Sacred Heart, St. Louis, Missouri; Brother Robert, OSB, Weston Priory, Weston, Vermont; Audrey Sorrento, Grailville, Loveland, Ohio; Judith Stoughton, CSJ, College of St. Catherine, St. Paul, Minnesota; Carroll Stuhlmueller, CP, Catholic Theological Union, Chicago; Paula Johannes, librarian of St. Mary of the Lake Seminary, Mundelein, Illinois. Timothy Slavin, from the office of Archives and Records for the archdiocese of Chicago, researched the dates of birth and death of the Chicago priests quoted in this book.

All of the librarians of the Catholic Theological Union, including Ken O'Malley, CP, Gerry Boberg, Jan Boyle, Debbie Cocanig, Frances Hankins, Juventino Lagos, Susie Mendoza, and Kate Skrebutenas, have responded to repeated requests for assistance with remarkable grace. Two students of the Catholic Theological Union, James Donohue, CR, and David Monaco, CP, served as research assistants and helped in the work of proofreading.

Frances Krumpelman, SCN, has been of invaluable assistance throughout the preparation of this manuscript: tracking down obscure quotations; researching biographical information about the pioneers; pointing out interesting parallels and converging ideas; typing and correcting the text; above all, keeping the project—and me—alive when I was bogged down with other work.

I am able to share my friends with you because Godfrey Diekmann shared his friends with me. For over ten years he has been mentor, colleague and friend. To him and to all of these people who have contributed to this collection in so many ways, my grateful thanks.

— *Kathleen Hughes,* RSCJ

KARL ADAM

1876–1966   Professor of dogmatic theology at Tuebingen;
one of the foremost theologians of his generation. English
translations of his books include: *One and Holy, Christ Our
Brother, The Spirit of Catholicism.* Of him Pascal Botz
said, "At his touch theology came to life. No one could possibly listen to him and remain untouched by the fire of faith
that illuminated his whole theology."

Christ in the liturgy

The worship of the church breathes the same spirit and is as much interwoven with Christ and full of Christ as is its morality. Just as every particular prayer of the liturgy ends with the ancient Christian formula, "through Christ our Lord," so is every single act of worship, from the Mass down to the least prayer, a memorial of Christ. Nay, more, the worship of the church is not merely a filial remembrance of Christ but a continual participation by visible mysterious signs in Jesus and his redemptive might, a refreshing touching of the hem of his garment, a liberating handling of his sacred wounds. That is the deepest purpose of the liturgy, namely, to make the redeeming grace of Christ present, visible and fruitful as a sacred and potent reality that fills the whole life of the Christian.

■ *THE SPIRIT OF CATHOLICISM, 1935*

Presence of Christ in the sacraments

The sacraments are nought else than a visible guarantee that Jesus is working in the midst of us. At all the important stages of our life, in its heights and in its depths, at the marriage-altar and the cradle, at the sickbed, in all the crises and shocks that may befall us, Jesus stands by us under the veils of the grace-giving sacraments as our friend and consoler, as the physician of soul and body, as our savior.

■ *THE SPIRIT OF CATHOLICISM, 1935*

Sacraments and human life

The church in her sacramental work embraces the inanimate creation, consecrating the altar stone, consecrating also the church's bells. We might speak of her rogation days whereon she blesses the produce of the fields. The whole of nature, the flowers of the field, the wax of the bee, the ears of corn, salt and incense, gold, precious stones and simple linen—there is nothing which she does not bring into the service of the sacred mystery, and bid them speak of it with their thousand tongues. Under her hands all nature becomes a "Lift up your hearts" and a "Bless ye the Lord." Where the [institutional] church herself is not active, there her children are at work. With hands that are rude and humble, but with eyes shining with the light of faith, they erect their sacred images and crucifixes in fields and by mountain paths and carry the light and consecration of the divine up to the soaring peak and down to the foaming torrent. Amid a Catholic folk and in a Catholic land—there statues of our Lady stand by the roadside, there the Angelus bell is heard.

■ *THE SPIRIT OF CATHOLICISM, 1935*

Through Christ our Lord

Faith in the Trinity is the basis for faith in the supernatural and consequently of the entire Christian system. Therefore, whenever our liturgy invokes the mediator, it at the same time addresses itself likewise to God "of whom and by whom and in whom are all things" (Romans 11:36). The Trinity is the true object of all liturgical worship. *Our liturgy is radically and essentially theocentric.* The liturgical prayers of the Mass were originally addressed directly solely to the Father, that is to say, to the Trinity through Christ. They all conformed to the ancient rule laid down in 393 by a synod of Hippo, at which St. Augustine was present: that all prayer be addressed to the Father. It was only in the course of centuries that, owing partially to the influence of the anti-Arian polemics, there crept even into the Roman Mass—liturgy prayers such as the Kyrie, the Gloria, the Agnus Dei, and the prayers preparatory to holy communion, which are not addressed directly to the Father but to Christ. Prayers to Christ used in private devotions were, however, known even in the primitive church (see Acts 7:59; Revelation 5:13; 7:10; 11:15). But speaking generally, the law of Hippo still holds. Only in exceptional circumstances, as on the feasts of Corpus Christi and of the Sacred Heart, does the liturgy of the Mass pray to Christ directly. Still less do we ever invoke the saints directly. It is always the triune God whom we beseech for help through the intercession of the saints. We may say, therefore, that however insistently the church in the liturgy stresses the *per Christum* [through Christ] idea, however unthinkable for her would be a Christianity without Christ, she nevertheless unhesitatingly proclaims that adoration and glorification of the Trinity is the final purpose, the *raison d'etre* of her worship because "of God and by God and in God are all things in heaven and on earth."

■ *ORATE FRATRES, 1937*

Liturgical prayer is communal prayer

It is no small merit of the liturgical movement that it has again and again emphasized how thoroughly the church's liturgy is pervaded with the idea of unity and community. Prayer in common, and for the community, prayer *pro vobis, pro multis* [for you (plural), for many] is essential to liturgical prayer, just as it was a characteristically basic trait of Jesus' praying. The eucharistic sacrifice likewise is first of all a community sacrifice. Not the individual alone, but the body of the faithful, the *cuncta familia* [whole family], the *plebs sancta* [holy people], offers itself to the Father in the

eucharistic *caro* [flesh]. It is a favorite thought of St.
Augustine that by partaking of the eucharistic *caro* we are
more closely united not only to Christ, but at the same time
to his Mystical Body as well. *Vos estis, quod accepistis* [You
are what you receive] (Sermon 227); *quod accipimus, nos
sumus* [what we receive, we are] (Sermon 229). In the eucharistic sacrifice, accordingly, it is not merely the *mysterium
Christi* [mystery of Christ] that is celebrated, but also that of
his Mystical Body, our own *mysterium*. Finally, it is well
known that from the very beginning the remaining sacraments were similarly considered as "social sacraments."

One thing is certain: If the idea of the supernatural community had always been fostered in the church's pastoral
work with the same understanding and the same love with
which it is inculcated by the liturgy, the enlightened individualism of the 18th and 19th centuries would have been
unable to penetrate even into ecclesiastical circles with such
devastating effects; we would likewise have been enabled
more readily and swiftly to harness with religious means
those movements of our own time in which the community
ideal asserts itself and becomes a driving force of an unparalleled intensity.

The path on which we are to meet God is open. God is
once and for all ours again, and we are God's. Hence the
basic Christian temper is that of hope and trust. Have confidence, my son, have confidence, my daughter! Where Christ
is, there can be no anxiety. "Why are you fearful, O ye of little faith?" (Matthew 8:26) "Peace be to you; it is I, fear
not." (Luke 24:36) And with confidence, thankfulness and
joy are conjoined. Christianity is a perpetual *Deo gratias*
[thanks be to God]. "Rejoice in the Lord always! Again I
say, rejoice." (Philippians 4:4)

In the spirit of this confidence, of this thankfulness and
joy, the church celebrates the sacrifice of Christ. Although
this sacrifice is primarily a memorial of the death and heroic
self-surrender of the Son of God, it is at the same time also a

remembrance of all the glory that blossomed forth from this death and resurrection. Wherefore too the cross which decorated the church's altars and the sign of the cross she weaves into the texture of her liturgy is not an expression of slavish dejection and of servile lowliness, but rather a symbol of her victory over the world and the ruler of the world, through Christ our Lord. The liturgy gives ample witness: Christianity is power, Christianity is consciousness of victory, is will to life, to eternal life—*per Christum dominum nostrum* [through Christ our Lord].

■ *ORATE FRATRES, 1937*

DONALD ATTWATER

1893–1977   Layman of St. Ives, Cornwall, England; associate editor of *Orate Fratres/Worship* from its beginnings in 1926 until 1958; expert on Eastern churches and liturgies; author of many works, including *Catholic Dictionary*. An able and forceful spokesperson for the laity, Attwater was also vigorous in promoting the vernacular.

Banishing jargon

We ordinary Catholics, without money, notoriety or influence, cannot stop the building of imitation Gothic or sham Baroque churches, or forbid the sale of imitation stained glass windows, nor hold up the publication of certain books of fiction, verse and devotion, nor censor the advertisements in some of our Catholic journals, nor banish aspidistras from under our altars or horrid and unecclesiastical music from our choirs; but we can quietly discourage the use of ecclesiastical jargon and by so doing help to keep from corruption that "innate grace and dignity of the Catholic mind" of which Cardinal Newman spoke, and which it seems part of the job of "progress and civilization" to destroy both in England and the United States.

■ *ORATE FRATRES, 1927*

A blaring of saxophones?

How to bring a better appreciation of the church's worship and its meaning to those who are necessarily obsessed by the demands of grinding work and the threat or actuality of an even more grinding poverty: Do we not shut our eyes to problems such as these? We do so at our peril.

I hope and believe that we are slowly in England making a body of people, clerical and lay, men and women, who are forming themselves for future activity. For we must *be* before we can *do*. Without personal *being,* all our *doing,* our activities, are as the crackling of flames under a pot, a sounding brass, a blaring of saxophones. We must know what we are trying to do and why. We must, each one of us for ourselves, lay hold of the salvation freely offered to us in the blood of the Lamb. We must have something of the mind of Christ. Only then, when we *are* something of the mind of Christ, can we hope to begin successfully to *do;* to begin to try to restore the beauty and dignity, the significant doing of sacred things on the Lord's day, Sunday, the day which the Lord has made. Let us be joyful and glad in it. Glad with the gladness of the overworked valiant women who, the Bible tells us, will laugh in the end of time, when the Lord Christ will come again in glory—that *parousia* we have heard so much about—to bring in the Sunday that shall have no end. How great, how glorious beyond human words, will be that day!

■ *Address at the National Liturgical Week, St. Louis, 1949*

To *hunt*, to *shoot*, to *entertain*

During the 12th century in the West a monastic notion was dominant, which defined the lay condition by state of life and saw it as a "concession"; it denied the laity any active part in the order of sacred things and sought to confine their activities wholly to temporal concerns. Then, in the following century, the canonical viewpoint became dominant and the layperson was defined as one who has no power of order and jurisdiction. And so on down to the 19th century, when the English Msgr. Galbot declared that the province of the laity is "to hunt, to shoot, to entertain. These matters they understand." And Cardinal Gasquet made the quip that "Laypersons kneel before the altar, sit below the pulpit—and put their hands into their purses."

Father [Yves] Congar contrasts such attitudes with the evidence about the state of thought and practice in earlier ages of the church and he eventually presents the laity as "Christians who are 'in the world,' there to do God's work insofar as it must be done in and through the work of the world."

■ *WORSHIP, 1956*

LAMBERT BEAUDUIN

1873–1960 Belgian monk of Mont César; called the "grand old man," the "heart and soul" of the liturgical movement which he initiated in Belgium in 1909; fellow monk of Columba Marmion; professor of apologetics, ecclesiology and liturgy at Sant' Anselmo, Rome, where he influenced American students; one of the founders of Centre Pastorale et Liturgique in Paris; played a decisive role in the birth of Catholic ecumenism; founder of the biritual monastery at Amay (later moved to Chevetogne); founder of the review, *Irenikon.* This tribute appeared in a Flemish newspaper: "Beauduin accomplished his goals not by a criticism of the church but by her interior renewal; not by separating but by seeking out everything which unites. A man of the church, the venerable figure of Dom Lambert Beauduin is present to our minds as the personification of the ancient church always renewing her youth in the full combat of the century."

The beauty of liturgical prayer

The church also teaches us the language we must use in speaking to God. It is in the liturgy that the magnificence of the divine Word is found. The liturgy is the supreme summit of poetry and thought. It speaks to God of the needs and infinite misery of people. If there is one thing that explains the desertion of a number of our churches by many Christians, it is certainly the insufficiency of the prayers which are substituted for the ancient, beautiful and traditional liturgy. On the day when the holy missal will stop being for many an unintelligible book, on the day when all will find again the key to what the priest says to God at the altar, a great number of those who have deserted the temples will return to them.

■ *Opening address at the Congress of Catholic Works, Belgium, 1909*

The power of liturgy

To those who understand what the liturgy is, the expectations of Pius X and of those who are endeavoring to promote his wishes in its regard will not seem exaggerated. The liturgy is the expression, in a solemn and public manner, of the beliefs, the loves, the aspirations, the hopes and the fears of the faithful in regard to God. It is not a cold, theoretical exposition of these things, as we have it in the catechism and theological books. It is the product of soul-stirring religious experience; it throbs with the life and warmth of the fire of the Holy Spirit, with whose very words it is replete and under whose inspiration it came into being. Like nothing else it has the power to stir the soul, to vivify it and to give it savor for the things of God. Its center is the holy eucharist and the other sacraments through which supernatural life and strength are imparted to the soul.

■ *LITURGY, THE LIFE OF THE CHURCH, 1926*

Liturgy is for all

What a shame that the liturgy remains the endowment of an elite; we are aristocrats of the liturgy; all people should be able to nourish themselves from it, even the simplest people: We must democratize the liturgy.

■ *A saying of Lambert Beauduin*

No aristocracy in the liturgy

The different states of prayer unfold themselves most wonderfully in the soul that is always united with our holy church. In fact, the liturgy recognizes many degrees of intensity, many different shadings. The light of one and the same sun is reflected with infinite variety, giving life to multicolored flowers that possess a charm forever new and to fruits as exquisite as they are various. It is outside these providential inequalities that the liturgical method glories in being popular and universal. Every child of the church is a saint in the making. *Hence this piety is not reserved exclusively for an ascetical aristocracy* and is not placed beyond the reach of ordinary Christians. All without distinction, from the pope to the smallest child learning the catechism, live the same liturgy in different degrees, participate in the same feasts, move in the same cycle. One can readily see what a powerful influence this unification of minds and hearts creates in the church.

■ *LITURGY, THE LIFE OF THE CHURCH, 1926*

The theology of the people

In contemplating the powerful structure of our Catholic cathedrals, do we ever think of all the laws of architectural technique, of all the scientific principles regarding the equilibrium and the resistance of various materials, of all the geometric theorems and algebraic formulas that are applied? Undoubtedly not. They are there nevertheless, regulating the entire construction, governing all the details of the shape and the place of every stone, thus assuring the stability and the preservation of the edifice. The eye does not discern them; hardly does the mind of the ordinary person suspect them; they are as the invisible soul of the body of stone. Thus it is with the liturgy. Dogma is everywhere, and it is not a mere part. It inspires and regulates the least gestures and least formulas, both with discretion and with minute care. The liturgy is theology, not scientifically expounded, but applied to the art of glorifying God and sanctifying people. The liturgy in turn renders two important services to dogma in the life of our holy church. It gives testimony of dogma, and its testimony is without appeal; it popularizes dogma by introducing it into the mind, the heart, the soul of the faithful with consummate pedagogical skill. It has been called the theology of the people.

■ *LITURGY, THE LIFE OF THE CHURCH, 1926*

What the liturgy is meant to do

Like the wonderful basilica, the liturgy has riches and splendors of infinite variety in reserve for all souls and for all circumstances of life. Yes! Would that the preachers explained it, the educators taught it, the theologians consulted it, men and women of action propagated it; that mothers and fathers spelled it out and children lisped it; that ascetics there learned true sacrifice; Christians, community and obedience; all humanity, true equality; and societies, harmony! May all Christians live it fully, come to draw the true Christian spirit at this "primary and indispensable source," and by means of living the liturgy, realize the prayer of the first Mass of the eternal high priest: that they be one—supreme wish and supreme hope!

That is the liturgical movement; all of that, nothing but that!

■ *LITURGY, THE LIFE OF THE CHURCH, 1926*

The risen Christ

I have told you many things. Forget everything; remember just this one thing: the risen Christ.

■ *At the closing of a retreat for Benedictine nuns, Belgium, 1940*

Tribute to Abbot Gueranger

Abbot Gueranger devoted himself without stint to restore the unknown riches of an ancient piety which the church has embedded deep in her liturgy. Such was the shining star that guided him providentially in all his ways. He envisaged this magnificent ideal under every one of its aspects. He was the professional liturgist in every sense of the word. The study and love of tradition and of liturgical institutions; the pastoral import of the liturgical year and of its multiple and varied teachings; the doctrinal foundations of that *locus theologicus* [theological source] of first importance; the treasures of asceticism and mysticism which the liturgical seasons and the lives of the saints bring us daily. In a word, Dom Gueranger was situated, as it were, in the center of the edifice, contemplating all its elements and facets. He is the liturgist without peer.

■ *ORATE FRATRES, 1948*

Reservation of the Blessed Sacrament

One did not reserve the blessed sacrament in order to adore it, but because it was reserved, it was adored.

■ *As quoted by Godfrey Diekmann in* WORSHIP, *1966*

Amen

Celui qui dit "Amen" en mourant est eternellement vivant. (The one who says "Amen" in dying lives eternally.)

■ *Near the end of his life*

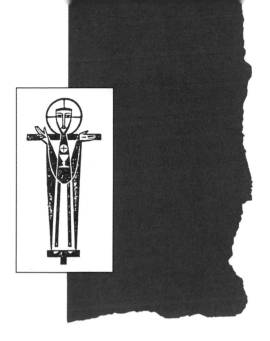

FLORENCE BERGER

1909–1983   Wife and mother; with husband, Alfred, was active in the National Catholic Rural Life Conference and the Grail; served on the board of the National Liturgical Conference; covered the second session of Vatican II for the *Catholic Telegraph* of Cincinnati; president of Cincinnati archdiocesan Council of Catholic Women; author of *Cooking for Christ,* a manual for introducing the celebrations of the liturgical year into the family. Florence and Alfred initiated a tape-of-the-month club that made talks and slides on matters liturgical available. They also taped the talks of the National Liturgical Conference for many years, beginning in 1958, and had 30 distribution centers for these materials.

Domestic church

To those of you who realize the all-important functions of the Christian home and know the liturgy as the first and greatest spiritual spring for quenching the bitter thirst of our parched, secular living: To you I pray. I do not pray that we theorize on theology but that together we find a thousand little ways of bridging the gap between principle and practice. I do not pray that we speculate on the nature of Christ and his mystical life today but that together we create a thousand situations in the family which make his life real to us and in us. I do not even pray that we contemplate the fresh and vital beauty of the liturgy with its roots in the past, its flower in the present and its tendrils reaching out to the future. But I do pray that together we can carry this beauty into a thousand homes where it will inspire young lives, give point to middle-age and yield a reward for long years of service. This I claim is woman's work—her share in the priesthood of Christ.

How is all this [the way family and friends celebrated the feast of the Holy Family] liturgy? Only insofar as the holy family lived in our house that day. Only insofar as the gathering of friends to sing and eat and act brought Christ and love in our midst. Only insofar as the scripture story became full and more real with the help of tradition. Only insofar as our prayer and song united us with Christ in the lifelong, sweet praise of God. Only that far was the liturgy brought home.

■ *Introduction to a series of articles on bringing liturgy into the home,* ORATE FRATRES, *1952*

Filling our homes with prayer

One author suggests that we set up "a prayer nook" in our homes which in time will become the very center of things. We in our family prefer to take family prayers out of "the nook" stage and consider all the house as holy. We have seen too much of the hiding away of the crucifix in the back bedroom. Too many "steal away to Jesus." I suppose if you could have one room set apart as a family chapel it would be very peaceful, but American apartments somehow forgot that extra room. In our case each time we managed an extra room by dint of building on, God sent an extra to fill it. Doesn't it seem that God wills to live in every room of our house? Should we not pray to God in every room of our house? Sometimes with more formality in choir formation, sometimes as children around our madonna, sometimes at ease at the table, or even over the pots and pans? Should not the sign of his cross be given a place of honor in the most honorable room, not in some hideaway? Then our house is marked as a house redeemed and our family as his chosen ones.

And in lieu of an altar we choose a dining table as he did, in lieu of formal altar cloth we choose a tablecloth which can express either feast or fast. For 30 years Christ chose to live in the intimacy of a home in Nazareth; it seems a pity to deny him any part of the houses where he lives today.

■ WORSHIP, 1952

ADE BETHUNE

1914— Born in Brussels, later moved to the United States; artist; founder-owner of St. Leo Shop in Newport, Rhode Island, a national resource for good liturgical art; contributor to the *Catholic Arts Quarterly* and other journals; artist for the *Catholic Worker.* Dorothy Day said this of her: "Whenever I visited Ade I came away with a renewed zest for life. She has such a sense of the sacramentality of life, the goodness of things, a sense that is translated in all her works whether it was illustrating a missal, making stained glass windows or sewing, cooking or gardening. To do things perfectly was always her aim. Another first principle she always taught was to aim high. 'If you are going to put a cross bar on an H,' she said, 'you have to aim *higher* than your sense of sight tells you.'"

Working saints

I thought it was only fitting to show working saints, since the paper was called *The Catholic Worker*. Then I began to realize there were no other saints. All saints were working saints. They were always busy with one or other of the 14 works of mercy, if not with several all at once. It took four years for me to understand the dignity of labor. It was not merely a consolation to the workers to know that the saints were workers too. It was a great dignity for the saints themselves to work. After all, the particular actions that the saints carried out were the same as the ones that we do all day long. So every work that we do can be a work of mercy and thus sanctified.

■ *Comments on the masthead she designed for*
THE CATHOLIC WORKER, *1940*

First, a reverence for food

E ating is a symbol of our salvation. It is a great symbol because it is a small symbol, a common symbol. We complain if it does not occur at least three square times, every day of our lives. It is intimately linked with our own dear selves. It is normally carried out in the merry company of others. At any rate, it is a common experience which we share with every human flesh that covers mortal bones. It is a true symbol of our union in and with God because it effects an organic union and assimilation.

N one of us can ever boast we love God as long as we hate our brother or sister. It is also true that no one can claim proper respect or devotion for the eucharist, unless we have first of all a proper reverence for food. It is all very well for us to go into pious raptures about the blessed sacrament and to kneel in church by the hour, reading reams of holy prayers, but it all won't ring quite true if at the same time we despise the ordinary food we eat, if we waste it, if we let it spoil, if we leave it on our plate and throw it in the garbage can.

God made us with the necessity of eating every day, and God supplies us with the food to eat. And what's more, the food which God gives us is delicious and we enjoy it. But, if we forget that all our food comes from God, that it is a gift from God, we will never treat it with the reverence that a gift from God deserves. Whether we buy our dinners from restaurants or chain stores or farmers, in cans, bottles, or cellophane, whether it come from wheat or corn or grape, or from cows or chickens, it all comes always as a gift from God.

As long as we forget that the blessed sacrament is primarily food, we will never understand what it means and we will never love it for what it is. Everything we eat is food. And therefore all of it is related, in a certain sense, to the bread and the wine of the eucharist, to the body of Christ and to the precious blood. For this we owe all food a special reverence, much in the same way as we have a special consideration for a great person's relatives, poor and insignificant though they may be, because they have a special share in his or her greatness.

Food that is given to another represents the giver. This is such a deeply rooted tradition of humankind that, although I may not be aware of the tradition, I will naturally feel hurt if my guests do not eat the food I give them. I feel they are refusing the gift of my friendship. If I like people, the first thing I shall do is to invite them for dinner, and, of course, I shall give them the best food that I am able to give them, because the food is not only for their need and their enjoyment, but it also stands for me. It is a gift of myself that I give to my guests.

And, after we have eaten the same food together, we find that we have become friends and the ice is officially broken, though we may have said little that was of any consequence. There is a real sense in which we become one because we have eaten the same food. So long as we have not a strong realization of the meaning of serving food to guests, we shall never understand the eucharist and we shall never love it for what it is; we shall never know that we are one because we eat one bread; we shall never be able to claim a true devotion to the blessed sacrament.

Who offers food, offers self. This is true of my giving a sandwich to a person at the door, or of my entertaining friends in the kitchen or the dining room. It is also true of banquets, where the servers are the ambassadors and representatives of the host who gives the food. It is true of farmers who raise food, of butchers who dress meats, of bakers who make bread, of grandmothers who put up preserves, of anyone who peels, cooks or prepares food for others. It is also true of every Christian who offers the bread and wine at the sacrifice of the Mass.

Eating food is an image of our assimilation to God. This makes eating a worthy work, and food an object of honor. Food is to be treated with respect, primarily, because it is a gift of God; in particular, because it is related to the matter of the eucharist; if for no other reason, because it is noble enough to nourish myself—a human being—and all other human beings; symbolically, because it represents the giver and because the one meal makes the guests one; and finally, because it is an image of our union with God.

■ *ORATE FRATRES, 1941*

Images of the Father

A mong traditional analogies found in Christian art across the centuries the hand is probably the most expressive and frequently used analogy of the Father. By the fourth century it is already a fully developed pictorial symbol based on numerous scriptural texts: "The souls of the just are in the hand of God" (Wisdom 3), "Humble yourselves under the mighty hand of God" (1 Peter 5) "You held me in your right hand" (Psalm 72), "You open your hand and fill every living creature with your blessing" (Psalm 144).

Primarily the hand means making—hence creation. It is also a symbol for the speaking mouth, since making is a sort of utterance, the work of our hands, an image or word.

Flowing from these thoughts is that of the hand as the giver of gifts, gifts representing the heart—that is, love. Conversely, it is also the hand which accepts offerings, and thus it stands also for the kindly ear receiving the sound of our prayers.

Finally, we think of hands as wings, as protection and as transmission of power in blessing. "Under God's wings you shall trust." (Psalm 90)

The sea also is symbolic of the Father, the Creator, thought of as either a father or mother, limitless, profound, brimming over with life and creative potential. The sea gives birth to living things. From the waters, too, we are reborn in holy baptism, while the Father seeing in us his own, exclaims: "This is my beloved child." The energy of torrent or mighty tempest destroys our work like matchsticks. But water also refreshes, restores, forgives and rejuvenates. "Oh the depth of the riches of the wisdom and the knowledge of God!" (Romans 11) "Drop down dew, ye heavens, from above, and let the clouds rain the just one." (Isaiah 45)

■ *WORSHIP, 1958*

The classical posture of prayer

The classical attitude, standing and arms outstretched, doubtless goes back to Christ and the apostles. Many of the earliest paintings in the catacombs show the figure of the *orante*, a young woman representing the praying soul, or the church, or Mary, standing in prayer with arms outstretched.

Try this experiment. Place your hands on your heart, then slowly stretch out your arms. You will feel that your heart is opening like a flower to speak to God. The lifting of the hands corresponds to "the raising of the mind and soul to God." Adoration is expressed by the open, defenseless heart; praise is expressed by the lifted arms. The open hands speak of thanksgiving, as if invisible thanks offerings were poised on each hand and lifted to the Lord. But the empty hands also represent human needs, and in this they stand for begging or petition.

■ *Explanation of one of her paintings, 1962*

BERNARD BOTTE

1893–1980   Monk of Mont César, Louvain; professor of Greek and scripture; collaborator at Centre Pastorale et Liturgique; founder of the ecumenical conferences at the Russian Orthodox Institute, Saint-Serge, Paris; director of the Institut de Liturgie, Paris, 1956–1964; editor of the critical edition of the classic *Apostolic Tradition of Hippolytus*. He inspired the insistence found in the *Constitution on the Sacred Liturgy* that efforts of the liturgical renewal would be futile without proper liturgical formation of priests.

Reading the gospel to the sick

Among the 40 priests on hand more than half were totally unaware that the *Roman Ritual* contained a section on visiting the sick, with gospel readings and special prayers. This was true because most used abbreviated diocesan rituals which omitted this section. My memory of this is all the more striking since a little afterward a curate from Walloon Brabant came to visit me and asked advice about a sick worker in his parish who was almost always bedridden. The priest went to see him regularly, but the sick man always acted disagreeably. Then, one day he found him completely changed. What had happened? He gave no other reason than a visit from the Jehovah's Witnesses who read the gospel to him. The sick man simply said, "Father, why haven't you ever spoken to me about all this?" The curate was disturbed and came to ask me if it was permitted to read the gospel in that way to the sick. I reassured him by referring him to the *Roman Ritual*. What a strange aberration among the Catholic clergy to replace the word of God by an empty chat.

■ *Recollection of a study session held at Vanves, 1948*

The language of the liturgy

Once the message of Jesus had passed the borders of Palestine it also had to adopt the form of the Greek gospels. You could say that Greek was the official language of the universal church. And yet, to the extent that the gospel moved deeper into different regions, the need for written translations into different languages was felt. Thus, we find already from the second century onward biblical versions in Latin, Syriac, Coptic, then Armenian, Georgian and Ethiopian. Liturgy underwent the same evolution, and naturally so since the Bible was the very basis of liturgy. Worship services were spent reading the Old Testament, the gospels, the writings of the apostles. The psalter was the songbook of the congregation. The church of the first centuries never dreamed of celebrating the mysteries of Christ in a tongue unknown to the people. On the contrary, as soon as it found an adequately evolved language which had a written form, it hastened to adopt it. If Latin became the liturgical language, it is not because it was a sacred language but because it was the living language of the Roman people.

■ *In his memoirs, 1973*

The conditions for liturgical reform

You don't make a Christian liturgy for people who know nothing of the Old and very little of the New Testaments. Without a renewal of catechesis and preaching, liturgical reform is doomed to failure.

■ *In his memoirs, 1973*

Liturgical renewal—a long view

As far as essentials are concerned, the reform has always remained faithful to the spirit of the liturgical movement. The reform, although the result of the liturgical movement, is above all else a starting point. It is a plan for the future, and it would be a risky illusion to expect immediate, spectacular results from it.

Such an illusion presupposes a rather simplistic idea of liturgical reform, one which views the reform as a set of recipes destined to make the Mass more attractive and to fill the churches which were beginning to empty. This is to commit oneself to a dangerous pragmatism whose only criterion is success: Everything is good which attracts crowds. This leads to an escalation of undertakings which go from a touching naiveté to the eccentric.

True liturgical reform has nothing to do with this sort of display. First of all, the reform cannot be separated from the doctrinal work of the Council since the liturgy must express in worship the faith of the church. During the Council the Fathers of Vatican II reflected on the question of the church because it is the theological problem of the 20th century, not only in Catholicism but in all Christian confessions. It is in the church that the plan of God for bringing us all together in Christ is to be accomplished. The Council Fathers returned to the sources of revelation and made a distinction between human routine and the authentic tradition which ensures continuity in the life of the church. The Council's desire was that this renewed faith in the church be expressed in the liturgy so that the liturgy could permeate the whole life of individuals and communities.

The will of the Council is affirmed in more than one place in the *Constitution on the Liturgy.* This is why the document asks that the word of God be widely proclaimed in the language of the people. This is why it recommends that the true nature and simplicity of the rites be made evident. The Council Fathers wanted a rather flexible reform, one allowing to the episcopal conferences a certain amount of freedom for adaptation. But the fathers of Vatican II especially insisted on a renewal of catechesis and preaching.

■ *In his memoirs, 1973*

Confirmation and holiness

I was sent a copy of a request to the Commission from several bishops in favor of postponing confirmation until 14. It was signed by several bishops from Eastern Europe, behind the Iron Curtain. Here's how they explained the situation. They experienced some difficulty in getting parents to send their children to catechism up till the time the children were 14. If confirmation were at this age, the parents would be obliged to send the children to catechism for fear of seeing the sacrament refused. This looked perfectly immoral to me. But since the question was sent by several bishops to the Commission, I was obliged to take sides.

I did so at the next meeting when I presented the two opposing theses. On the one side there was the Roman tradition based on a theology of confirmation: It is the second stage of Christian initiation and cannot be delayed beyond the age of seven since the gift of the Spirit may be needed from the age of reason. On the other side there was a theory based on a debatable psychology which results in some absurd conclusions, such as delaying the sacrament till as late as the age of 18. The two theses do not have equal value. I concluded with two questions: "Can you affirm in your soul and conscience that confirmation is useless to children before 14? Can you assume the responsibility of depriving children of the grace of the sacrament for seven to ten years, especially in dechristianized lands and in those of concealed persecution?" I waited a few seconds, but no one answered "yes" to my two questions.

The most important reform was that of the sacramental formula. I proposed adopting the old formula of the Byzantine rite, a formula whose foremost quality was its biblical inspiration: "Seal of the gift of the Holy Spirit." The image of a mark, a seal, "sphragis," to designate the action of the Holy Spirit in Christian initiation comes from St. Paul in the epistle to the Ephesians (1:13) in the verbal form of "you have been sealed." It was widely used by the fathers of the church. The Byzantine formula, the most ancient of those in use today, is explicitly cited in a document attributed to the Council of Constantinople in 381, but actually dating from 450. With some variants, it is found in other Oriental rites. Thus it has a solid basis in tradition.

The proposal was well received, there being no opposition to it. For a translation I proposed: "Be sealed with the Holy Spirit who is given to you." This was approved by the Commission.

■ *Memories of participating in the revision of the rite of confirmation*

The most serious problem of the reform

I believe in the power of God's word. When it doesn't encounter obstacles, it grows irresistibly and produces a hundredfold. There is much good earth which is eager to open itself to the sowing of God's word, but we must provide this word. This is the request of the Council: preaching inspired by the word of God which clarifies and nourishes the faith of the people. In my opinion this is the most serious problem of the liturgical reform. The rest is secondary. I hope that those responsible would become more and more aware of this.

■ *Memories of participating in the revision of the rite of confirmation*

PASCAL BOTZ

1905– Monk of St. John's Abbey, Collegeville; graduate of the University of Tuebingen where he was a student of Karl Adam; collaborator of Virgil Michel on *Orate Fratres;* professor of dogmatic theology at St. John's Seminary; editor of *Sponsa Regis;* one of the compilers of *A Short Breviary,* published by The Liturgical Press in 1941.

The dynamic appeal of the liturgy

The liturgical apostolate is destined to grow in proportion as Christians recognize that the liturgy fills a primary need in their religious lives. The perennial strength of the movement consists in its dynamic, vital appeal more than in publicity or even literary attempts to sponsor it. The spirit of this revival takes hold of individuals as soon as they renew their interior selves according to certain objective norms of corporate Christian living; therefore the liturgical movement is less dependent on the force of high-powered propaganda or on leadership by magnetic personalities than are secular movements and is less affected by the vicissitudes of human enthusiasm and inspiration. Genuine liturgical reform is the work of God, our cooperation being a necessary condition.

■ *ORATE FRATRES, 1936*

Purple patches

Renovamini spiritu! [Be renewed in spirit!] This strikes the keynote of all observances performed in the spirit of Lent, which is the time for renewing one's innermost self. Lenten practices affect the heart through the senses and therefore conform to the church's sacramental system which elevates the interior person by means of visible signs. Few people think of doing penance in order to acquire the liturgical spirit, this "most Catholic" spirit, because they fail to understand the true purpose of all penance. How gratefully would modern Christians look back over the 40 days of Lent if on Holy Saturday they had escaped from the spirit of individualism and gained in corporate consciousness by having taken the point of view of the church in her lenten liturgy! How much stronger would they feel for having fasted and prayed as members of a spiritual organism rather than as separate entities!

A sceticism with a view to one's needs as a member of the mystic body reveals the folly of the usual post-Lenten relaxation, when so many faithful retire their unbroken resolutions into the attic of their penitential past. Cessation of mortification is, after all, a most certain sign that practices have affected the individual, but superficially and not vitally. Purple patches! A violet patch on a nonlenten pattern can well bear removal after it has served as an emblem of penance. But it is the everyday garb that matters to those who understand that self-denial cannot be divorced from daily striving after virtue. Practices which one can discard with impunity had better be thrown away, because they are not born of actual conditions or of necessity but are fictitious products of an inventive mind. "Resolutions" ought to fit real life conditions; otherwise they are fashions of the season, distinctly modern indeed, but subjective and unsocial in character.

O ur membership in the Mystical Body of Christ is the basis for optimism even while practicing penance. Such is our solidarity in Christ that nothing, not even the "individual's act of resistance to temptation," is private. One member denies himself or herself and the corporate body profits. If this be so, how decidedly ought not a Christian's social sense suggest the line of action for the season of Lent! Rather than flee into privacy, we ought to seek others to come under our influence, to keep eyes and ears and hands open to the needs of neighbor. "Deal thy bread to the hungry; give shelter" and "whatsoever you do to the least of these . . ." mean that "penitents" may not look for their own will in their ascetical practices. And loving one's enemy is always a denial of self-will. Charity is not so much an attitude as a practice, one which helps "purify the church," as the oration of the First Sunday of Lent puts it.

■ *ORATE FRATRES, 1936*

Breathing the air of divine truth

The divine Christ-life is the unchangeable content of the liturgy presented in the ever-changing garb of seasons and feasts and hours.

The liturgy is the greatest teacher of the truths we believe. It gives the proper balance and setting to faith in the life of a Christian by incorporating the creed and all revealed truths into everyday prayer and worship. The form of truth as proposed by the liturgy is not, indeed, the conventional form of theses, propositions and corollaries, but (because the liturgy is faith lived, prayed and chanted) it varies the presentation of truths by means of hymns, orations, prefaces, readings from the epistles and gospels, psalms, even external rites and gestures, painting and architecture. What Catholic, who follows the church in her prayer life, does not continually breathe the atmosphere of divine truth: the priority of grace over human initiative; the universal efficacy of the incarnation, passion and resurrection of Christ; our oneness in Christ; the intercession of the Blessed Virgin and the communion of saints; the necessity of dying to sin and rising to a new life; the function of the virtues and gifts of the Holy Ghost? And what is more: These truths are not abstract in the liturgy, but are truths enriching life, for the liturgy is life-giving.

■ *ORATE FRATRES, 1936*

The gospel

The word of the gospel in the Mass is never detached from Christ its author. He himself, who is present in his Mystical Body, addresses his faithful members through his visible minister of the word. He continues to do what he did of old: mediate life and truth, only now it follows the sacramental economy of visible ministers. For that reason and because of the efficacy of his word, the gospel has been called the audible sacrament.

■ *ORATE FRATRES, 1942*

Karl Adam's gift to the world

One day, when eating at Karl Adam's house, he sliced a piece of bread for me from a loaf that, European fashion, lay on his table. I remarked to him on the clean cut he had made and that it was symbolic of his thinking. He smiled and graciously spoke from his heart about the need of going to the essence of things, of seeing parts in relation to the whole, of fearless devotion to truth, even to its last hiding place, of the need for clear-cut scientific method over against so much loose thinking in our day. Since then I have realized how he, too, has fed the multitudes of the world, and how well they have fared with the bread of his theology.

■ *WORSHIP, 1958*

LOUIS BOUYER

1913– Member of the Oratory; professor of spiritual theology at Institut Catholique, Paris; authority in fields of spirituality and ecumenism; his books include *Liturgical Piety, Life and Liturgy, Rite and Man, The Fourth Gospel, Eucharist;* member of the summer faculty of liturgy assembled at Notre Dame by Michael Mathis. Like Tertullian, one would not predict which side of an issue he might take at the podium.

No easy compromise

It is to this world that we are to give witness of the divine *agape*, in order to snatch out of its power the children of God who are there enslaved and bring them into liberty. But this task can only be accomplished by means of our cross and theirs, borne patiently and even joyfully as being Christ's own cross. And thus we shall come to the resurrection, where everything that we had to lose in order to follow Christ will be found once more in the new *kosmos*, the new order of things and of being, where he is king, having overcome Satan and thrust his power down to hell.

We must frankly acknowledge that this view of reality, which gave no difficulty to the Christians of antiquity, seems very hard for us to face today; it is not at all easy for our mind to accept it. But we need to face it quietly and try to understand it more perfectly, for unquestionably this view of reality underlies the whole Catholic liturgy and is the prerequisite to any true understanding of the central mystery of the liturgy. We cannot attempt once more to live a full liturgical life and at the same time be able to dismiss this view as one that is too gloomy and fanatical to be taken by any modern, well-educated and sensible Christians. And we must not deceive ourselves with the hope of finding some easy compromise which would enable us to continue in our comfortable attitude toward this world, while accepting the view of it expressed in the Bible and the liturgy only in such a way as to make it more palatable.

■ *LITURGICAL PIETY, 1955*

Word and sacrament

The word of God the church has to bring to the world cannot be merely a kind of instruction. Nor can its highest expression be found in teaching, in preaching, as if all that came after merely repeated, on a lower plane, what was already said more exactly by purely oral and intelligible means. The word that is simply listened to, since it is the word of God, tends of itself to become an event, an event of our life in which the divine life encounters and possesses it. This divine fact, which comes to meet us by taking into itself our own personal acts, is precisely what, according to the teaching and practice of the Catholic church, the sacrament is, and this is perfectly in accord with the teachings of St. Paul and St. John.

■ *THE WORD, CHURCH, AND SACRAMENTS: IN PROTESTANTISM AND CATHOLICISM, 1960*

The eucharist makes the church

The eucharistic prayer, which is adhesion to the word made flesh, in its total sense, consecrates the messianic banquet in which God's gift is completed, which is made to us in Christ, so that all may become one body and one spirit: *his* body animated by *his* spirit.

It is in this way that the church is made and unceasingly maintained through the Mass, for the Mass is the assembly in which the evangelical word is proclaimed, the Christian faith confessed, the bread broken, the cup shared, which this word and the prayer that receives it have consecrated— where the parousia is therefore hoped for, the coming of the reign is besought and accelerated. This is to say that the Mass is, and is only, the church in act, the church becoming, sustaining and developing itself without ceasing. This does not mean, as the Second Vatican Council specified, that the Mass, the eucharistic liturgy, exhausts in itself the life of the church. It is the center, source and summit of that life: the summit toward which all evangelization tends, the witness given to the word and, first of all, the faith which receives it—the source in which are nourished prayer and charity, which must fill individual and collective Christian existence and prepare the world by preparing us for salvation, for judgment and for the reign of God.

■ *THE CHURCH OF GOD, 1970*

To have a common life

Whoever says "communion in charity," in the powerfully realistic vision of the New Testament, says *a fortiori* "community of life," and to be capable of having a common life we must begin by living it together. Charity or communion in charity is not an abstract convergence of completely interior sentiments; it is a sharing of the whole of human life, in and by which are united, not by desire or intention but "in fact," hearts into which the same spirit has been poured from on high. Again, if the Spirit has been poured on *together,* it is because they *were all together.* The realism, essential to New Testament spirituality and therefore to the church, which we see being formed in it, finds its touchstone in the gospel notion of "neighbor."

■ *THE CHURCH OF GOD, 1970*

WILLIAM BUSCH

1882–1971   Born in Red Wing, Minnesota; studied church history at Louvain; professor of church history at St. Paul Seminary in Minnesota for more than 50 years; advisor and guide to Virgil Michel; associate editor of *Orate Fratres* for more than two decades; translator of books by Parsch and others; supporter of the National Liturgical Weeks from 1940 on. Busch was esteemed as the elder statesman of the liturgical movement; he inspired a whole generation of priests by the liturgical digressions (which his students in church history would contrive to have him make more frequently). In 1919, in a letter in *Ecclesiastical Review,* he advocated "an altar of wood with four legs, the simple table of the Last Supper . . . the essential table."

Liturgy and modern individualism

Undoubtedly there is something amiss in the present quality of Catholic spirituality. Our devotional life, and hence our whole mentality as Catholics, is individualistic, and the chief reason for this is to be found in an examination of our prayer books. The individualistic character of modern prayer literature cannot fail to impress itself upon our life and to dim our social vision. But the official liturgical prayers of the church, which we do not use, or which we use so privately and mechanically as not to count, are filled through and through with that very spirit for which you are so justly pleading. We have lost that sense of Christian neighborliness and of the kingdom of God on earth which the liturgy teaches.

The committee which has been formed "to study the causes of Catholic apathy" will not find any cause more deep-seated and far-reaching than this fundamental one which I here suggest, namely—the neglect of the liturgy, the expression of the common mind and heart of the *ecclesia Dei*. And no remedy for the apathy which you deplore is more worthy of study than is the present liturgical movement in all the Catholic parts of Europe.

■ *Letter to the editor of* COMMONWEAL, *1925*

Liturgy and life

We all share, at Mass, in the priesthood and in the victimship of Christ, but this incorporation is of little value if it ceases to function the moment we step out onto the church porch.

■ *Letter to Godfrey Diekmann, 1940*

The liturgical movement in historical perspective

The liturgical movement is not a fad such as springs up suddenly and flourishes for a short time. The pace of its growth has been not unlike that of previous liturgical movements in the church's history.

For, if you will look back into history, you will observe that such movements have come periodically, say about every 500 years. First of all, there was the primitive movement of the apostolic age. In order to recognize that it was liturgical movement, we have only to consult the Acts of the Apostles and the Epistles and the Apocalypse. Next, if you travel down about 500 years, you will meet the name of St. Benedict and that of Pope Gregory I, whose name is attached to the Gregorian sacramentary and to Gregorian chant. Another 500 years will bring you to the Cluny movement, which certainly was liturgical, and to the reforms of Pope Gregory VII. Still another 500 years, and we reach the Council of Trent and Pope Pius V and the reforms which gave us our present text of the liturgical books. And finally, another 500 years bring us to Pope Pius X and to our present liturgical movement. We see, therefore, that our present liturgical movement is not something "impossible" — it is something inevitable.

Moreover you will observe that these earlier movements all extended over at least 100 years, so that by comparison our present one will not reach its height until another 50 years from now. We are called to do our part in it, and let us not lose time. Let us be prompt in corresponding to the graces of the Holy Spirit. But let us not be hasty. None of these movements in the church's history were wrought out in a short time. Let us know well what we are about; let us understand well the meaning of this great event. It is not merely a matter of our personal efforts; it is a movement in the life of the church of which we are members.

■ *Address at the first National Liturgical Week, Chicago, 1940*

The inner meaning of the liturgy

I n time all of the faithful will be instructed in the inner
meaning of the liturgy, upon which the encyclical insists
so distinctly, and [they] will be enabled to exercise, not only
in external ways, but in mind and heart, with intelligence
and devotion, that active participation in the sacred mysteries and in the solemn public prayer of the church which is
"the primary and indispensable source of the true Christian
spirit."

■ *Reflections on* MEDIATOR DEI *in* ORATE FRATRES, *1948*

PAUL BUSSARD

1905–1983   Priest of the archdiocese of St. Paul; student of
William Busch; one of Virgil Michel's most faithful collab-
orators; associate editor of *Orate Fratres/Worship* for many
years; in 1930, founder and editor-in-chief of *The Leaflet
Missal,* which by 1955 had sold 30 million copies; author of
Vernacular Missal; editor-in-chief of *Catholic Digest.*

"The Lord be with you"

The Lord be with you." The words themselves are very ancient. You will find them in several places in the Old Testament. In the Book of Ruth, for example, they are a greeting. Ruth went out to the field to glean corn. The owner of the field came out also and said to the reapers, "The Lord be with you." And they answered him, "The Lord bless you" (Ruth 2:4). We are all familiar with the way the angel greeted the Blessed Virgin, "Hail, full of grace, the Lord is with you" (Luke 1:28). Mary was, in the most profound sense of the word, the first member of the church. In her Christ lived. Now there are many members of the church and in them Christ lives through sanctifying grace. Thus is the prophecy of Isaiah (7:14) fulfilled, "Behold a virgin shall conceive and bear a son, and his name shall be called Emmanuel" (God with us).

■ *THE MEANING OF THE MASS, 1942*

Incensing

What is the meaning of the incense? That which is most evident is that the incense represents our prayers. This is pointed out by the blessing and by the prayers said during the incensing. We may develop the symbolism a bit. Incense arises because the grains of incense are placed upon burning charcoal. Where there is no fire there is naturally no incense rising up in curling clouds and diffusing the odor of adoration. Our prayers are like that. They must come from a heart "on fire with love," that is, one must be a living member of the body of Christ, a temple of the Holy Ghost if one's prayers are to ascend to heaven diffusing the sweet-smelling odor of adoration.

But the incensing has another meaning. Incense is a mark of honor. Thus the censer bearer walks at the head of processions. Incense was put to this use from the remotest antiquity. When the gifts are incensed, the action indicates the honor and dignity which they have by reason of their role in the sacrifice. The altar is incensed next, because it, too, has great honor and dignity as a symbol of Christ. Then the celebrant is incensed because it is through his priestly power that Christ acts. Then the ministers, because each of them has something to do, and finally the community, because of its dignity, for the members of the community are members of Christ offering with him to God their life and love.

■ *THE MEANING OF THE MASS, 1942*

DANIEL CANTWELL

1914— Student of Reynold Hillenbrand; priest of Chicago; pastor; seminary professor who taught sociology and the theological bases of the liturgy. Cantwell was the founder of the Chicago Catholic Interracial Council, Friendship House and the Catholic Labor Alliance and was the full-time chaplain to these lay groups for two decades. He was a frequent public speaker, not only in Catholic churches, but in union halls, universities and other churches. He said recently, "My own thrust was not in the social movement as such but to free up the laity to spread the kingdom of God. And the laity have done that. It was an effort 50 years ago. We often worked in isolation. It seems utterly preposterous now that we had to take that approach, but that's the way it was."

What is Sunday?

What was Sunday intended to be? We can probably best find the church's answer to this in the Divine Office.

From Evening Prayer on Saturday to Evening Prayer on Sunday we are constantly told what Sunday is intended to be. It is the day that is overshadowed with the majesty of God, God's wisdom and God's ways. Evening Prayer on Saturday ushers in the spirit of Sunday for us with: "O the depth of the riches of the wisdom and of the knowledge of God! How incomprehensible are God's judgments, and how unsearchable are God's ways."

It is the day for knowing God as God best likes to be known: the God of love, to serve whom it is necessary also to love. In the middle of Sunday morning that lesson is given to us: "God is charity; and all who abide in charity, abide in God, and God in them."

It is the day for coming to love each other more, for greater unity and peace among us. At Midday Prayer we carry away the lesson: "Bear ye one another's burdens, so you shall fulfill the law of Christ."

It is the day for knowing the dignity of what we are and what we do, and for preparing to bear the labor of the week. As Sunday begins to draw to a close we are told in prayer in midafternoon: "You are bought with a great price. Glorify and bear God in your body."

It is the day for rediscovering the parental care of God for us, God's providence in our weakness. At Sunday Evening Prayer our hearts are raised up with the great truth: "Blessed be the God and Father of our Lord Jesus Christ, the Father of mercies, and the God of all comfort, who comforts us in all our tribulation."

Sunday, then, is the Lord's Day. It belongs to God. We freely give it to God. God has it coming in justice, God who made all the other days and all that the heavens and earth contain. It is the day for giving to God the acknowledgment God deserves, the praise and the glory. It is the day of sacrifice, of community gift-giving, when Christ and his brothers and sisters in community renew the sacrifice of Calvary for the foremost reason of telling our God: "How great we know you are, how wonderful, how good!"

■ *Address at the National Liturgical Week, St. Louis, 1949*

Sunday and social concern

There is a danger which can arise from too exclusive an emphasis on the sanctification of the Lord's Day. Such an emphasis can give the impression that liturgical reform is something of an escape from attacking the hard social problems which face working people every day of the week. The impression can also be given that somehow the other days of the week do not belong to the Lord, or that religion is not concerned with them.

Indeed we might seriously consider whether it is possible to restore all things in Christ on Sunday until we first show ourselves equally concerned with the necessity of restoring to the working lives of the multitudes their Christian dignity and human rights. For them, religion and worship, as they know them, have become aloof and distasteful. For them, what has happened to Sunday differs not at all from what has happened to the other days of the week. If there is nothing to make them conscious of their priesthood with Christ on Sunday and make them want to worship, there is also nothing in the socioeconomic life of the other days of the week to remind them of their kinship with Christ in the affairs of the temporal order.

It is not hard to understand the answer which a girl working in the slums of Chicago gave to my question: What has happened to Sunday? She spontaneously remarked: "I can think of many more important questions." While her answer may sound flippant, I'm sure Abbé Godin and Abbé Michonneau in the Parish Mission of France would have understood what she meant.

The lapsed Christian—in the United States and in France—cannot be forgotten. Sunday must be restored to them and they to the Christian community. But we can only do so by restoring the whole God, God who is as concerned about their daily lives and human problems as about Sunday; who not only lays down laws of worship and morality but who gives rights and dignity to us all and decrees that to violate them is to violate God; who hates economic injustice, racial tyranny and prejudice, international isolationism, low wages meted out to workers, the enormous inequity in the distribution of created wealth, inhuman working conditions, and selfish unconcern for the problems of other people; who hates all these things even more vigorously than mute congregations and poorly sung chant.

If around the altar we fill the minds of the people with both their dignity as priests with Christ and their rights as kings with Christ, Sunday will come to life again. It will be evident that the great God has made it. Spontaneously all will rejoice and be glad in it.

■ *Address at the National Liturgical Week, St. Louis, 1949*

JOHN CARROLL

1735–1815   Born into a moderately wealthy Maryland family; educated at St. Omer, the college of the English Jesuits in Flanders; entered the Society of Jesus, 1753; returned to America after ordination and ministered with the Jesuits in Maryland; consecrated first Bishop of Baltimore August 15, 1790, a diocese that extended roughly from the Atlantic to the Mississippi. His election as first United States bishop by his fellow priests was confirmed by Rome on November 6, 1789. One of his biographers reflected on his 25 years as bishop: "He seemed quite oblivious to his own part in the enormous progress Catholicism had made. The laity had increased four times over; the clergy had been more than doubled. He left three seminaries, three colleges for men (among them Georgetown University) and several academies for young women. There were three convents for women and three religious orders of men well established, and the Sisters of Charity were spreading all through the East. But far more important than these signs of physical growth, the age of Carroll in the American church firmly fixed the traditions which were to ennoble and to augment the prestige of that organization. Carroll's unabating devotion to religious freedom put the Catholic church squarely on the side of justice and civil liberties in the public mind. His careful delineation of the relations of the church with Rome in spiritual matters dispelled any doubt about the Catholic's loyalty to the nation in political affairs. He was the *beau ideal* of patriot and priest to all who knew him. He achieved collaboration rather than competition between clergy and laity. He was the *pastor bonus* [good shepherd] of the American church in its infancy." (Melville, *John Carroll of Baltimore* [New York: Scribner's & Sons, 1955], 285–87)

Vernacular

The great part of our congregations must be utterly ignorant of the meaning and sense of the public offices of the church. It may have been prudent, for aught I know, to refuse a compliance with the insulting and reproachful demands of the first reformers [the 16th century Protestants who insisted on vernacular liturgies]; but to continue the practice of the Latin liturgy in the present state of things must be owing either to chimerical fears of innovation or to indolence and inattention in the first pastors of the national churches in not joining to solicit or indeed ordain this necessary alteration.

■ *Letter written in 1787 or 1788*

THOMAS CARROLL

1910–1971 Priest of the archdiocese of Boston; received national recognition for innovative leadership in the apostolate to the blind, his lifelong ministry; in 1945, elected president of the Liturgical Conference, an office he held for four colorful terms; contributed to making Liturgical Weeks significant national events. He refused the title of monsignor until Archbishop Cushing, on Carroll's 25th anniversary of ordination, went to the center for the blind, served the Mass at which Carroll presided, then insisted that he accept the title. A colleague said of him that he was a wonderful, tall, handsome, cheerful Irishman, very friendly, a marvelous host, all heart, not a scholar but a good pastor, and just what the liturgical movement needed among its leaders.

Some progress

We are old people now in this apostolate—many of us. And in our years we have seen many things. In one decade, we have seen an end to the vocal opposition to the apostolate. We have seen the widespread dawning of the knowledge that the sacred liturgy does not mean rubrics, ceremonies and arty display. We have seen a tremendous spur given to the younger priests, the sisters and the seminarians. We have seen the laity awakened by the voice of the sovereign pontiff to a thirsting for the participation which he says should be theirs. We have seen the dogmatic theologians coming to the forefront of the movement (and the beginning of the revision of theological textbooks to comprehend it). We have seen the start of a whole new development of ascetical theology—which will still bear individual sanctification foremost in mind, but will make that individual sanctification more clearly the sanctification of the individual member of the body of Christ.

■ *Address at the National Liturgical Week, Grand Rapids, 1953*

The liturgical apostolate

Pius XII is the pope of the sacred liturgy. To him it is not a petrified thing—as the church is not a petrified thing. It is the public prayer of the family of God. It is not an exclusive thing, but a part—and the foremost part—of the prayer of the Christian. It is not antithetical to private prayer—and any thought that it would rule out private prayer, meditation or contemplation is not papal thought, not Christian thought.

To Pius XII, the sacred liturgy is something for the people even as the church is for the people. And this is something that all of us must remember—he not only suggests, he insists that their part must be recognized. To this pope of individual sanctification and apostolic activity, the liturgical movement has ceased to be a "movement." He calls it rather what we have called it today. To him it is an "apostolate." He brings the sacred liturgy to the people in order that it may bring the people to Christ.

An earlier Pius—the sainted Pius V—protected the sacred liturgy from hostile hands and gave to it a historical "fixation," a "setting," a sort of period of "suspended animation," a stage of suspended development—so that in the sweeping currents of Reformation and counter Reformation it might not suffer deformation.

The Blessed Pius X brought it forth from its place of protection in order that again it might grow as it was needed by a new age.

And now the glorious Pius XII—to whom the church is *for the people,* and its sacred liturgy *for the people*—has suddenly and with amazing rapidity given to it new development.

■ *Address at the National Liturgical Week, Grand Rapids, 1953*

ODO CASEL

1886–1948   Monk of Maria Laach, student of Idlefons Herwegen; chaplain for Benedictine sisters; founder and editor of *Jahrbuch fuer Liturgiewissenschaft;* with Romano Guardini, edited *Handbuch fuer Liturgiewissenschaft;* formulated his *mysterium* theology, the "mystical making-present again" of the total work of redemption in the liturgical rites of the sacraments. A memorial tribute in *Orate Fratres* commented on "the enormous achievement of this quiet monk who never traveled, never lectured, and never produced anything but 'occasional' books, slim in size; who loved solitude and enjoyed company; practiced silence and had more to say than anybody else when he spoke; who preached the glorious Christ and was deeply attached to the mystery of the cross. He founded an entirely new school of liturgical and historical research." He died Easter night when he had just finished proclaiming "Lumen Christi" and was ready to intone the Exsultet.

The mystery of worship

The Greek word "liturgy" originally meant the act of an individual in the service of the city; for example, fitting up a ship for war or sponsoring a choir for the tragedies in honor of Dionysius; service generally, and in particular the service of God in public worship. In this sense it is used by Old and New Testament.

When we place the words "mystery" and "liturgy" side by side, and take mystery as mystery of worship, they will mean the same thing considered from two different points of view. Mystery means the heart of the action, that is to say, the redeeming work of the risen Lord, through the sacred actions he has appointed; liturgy, corresponding to its original sense of "people's work," "service," means rather the action of the church in conjunction with this saving action of Christ's.

■ *THE CHRISTIAN MYSTERY, 1930*

Liturgy and symbol

In the Greco-Roman world, clothing was not a casual or indifferent matter; with a new garment went a new identity. In the mysteries a garment or a sign of the god was put on, and the initiate became that god. In connection with these customs, Paul cries out, "All of you who have been baptized in Christ, have put on Christ." In Easter week the church sings this of the baptized who stand about the altar in their white clothing. This example shows us once more that some customs which signify a mystical uniting with the godhead were particularly well appointed to serve the Christ-mysticism of the liturgy. Thus the age-old idea of representing the embodiment of divine strength with food and drink is brought up to its highest pitch of reality by the eucharist: a real meal with God, representing our deepest union with the God-man and rendering it fact, as the Lord himself says of it in John 6.

■ *THE CHRISTIAN MYSTERY, 1930*

The church year

When the church year celebrates historical occurrences and developments, it does not do so for its own sake but for that of eternity hid within it. The great deed of God upon us, the redeeming work of Christ which wills to lead us out of the narrow bounds of time into the broad spaces of eternity, is its content.

Yet this content is not a gradual unfolding in the sense that the year of nature naturally develops; rather, there is a single divine act which demands and finds gradual accustoming on our part, though in itself complete. When the church year fashions and forms a kind of unfolding of the mystery of Christ, that does not mean it seeks to provide historical drama but that it will aid us in our step-by-step approach to God, an approach first made in God's own revelation. It is the entire saving mystery that is before the eyes of the church and the Christian, more concretely on each occasion. We celebrate Advent, not by putting ourselves back into the state of unredeemed humankind, but in the certainty of the Lord who has already appeared to us, for whom we must prepare our souls; the longing of ancient piety is our model and teacher. We do not celebrate Lent as if we had never been redeemed, but as having the stamp of the cross upon us, and now only seeking to be better conformed to the death of Christ, so that the resurrection may be always more clearly shown upon us.

■ *THE CHURCH'S SACRED YEAR, 1931*

DOROTHY CODDINGTON

1912– Born in New York City; living now in Chicago; wife and mother of four; editor of *The Catholic Worker,* 1933–1936; friend of Dorothy Day and Virgil Michel; with her husband, Albert (Tom), founded and edited the journal, *Liturgy and Sociology,* 1936–1939; contributor to *Orate Fratres;* worked at *Time* magazine, 1942–1944; author of *Glory to God,* 1951; editor (at various companies and freelance) of medical and educational publications for many years. She is the sole survivor of the first years of the Catholic Worker movement.

Teaching children the meaning of baptism

L et me cite the instance of a little girl who had not yet
received her first communion but at the beginning of
Lent said, "I received the Holy Ghost when I was baptized,
and that's why we do things for Lent, because we die with
Christ and rise with him."

The explanation of her very Pauline theology, which was
far beyond what she had been taught in school, lay in the
fact that she had been given, as a baby, one of Ade Bethune's
lovely baptismal certificates, giving the facts of her baptism
and quoting St. Paul. This had hung on the wall of her room
and had been one of her treasured possessions. Each night
when she was going to bed she insisted on her mother reading the certificate to her and answering, again and again, her
questions about her baptism.

From the time they were very small, the children of this
family had taken part in an annual ceremony of the renewal
of their baptism, which included going through the entire
ritual of baptism in the baptistry of their church. Moreover,
the symbols used by Bethune—the water and the candle—
were familiar to this child by constant use in the "home liturgy"; holy water was in frequent use in the home, and she
was accustomed to seeing the holy candle lit during the Saturday night reading of the next day's gospel, because "the
gospel is Christ."

■ *ORATE FRATRES, 1945*

Catechesis for children

Can children understand the psalms at an early age? Probably not; at least, they may not comprehend as their elders think they do. But I prefer to cut children's spiritual garments a little large, for them to grow into, as they will in time. And who knows what vivid image or hint of the beauty of God may remain in their mind and memory? Everyone who has dealt with children knows that they sometimes have remarkable insights into spiritual truths that theologians take many volumes to expound.

As children grow older and more able to understand in our grown-up way, we can, of course, enrich that understanding with broader knowledge. The church's use of the psalms in the liturgy provides the perfect basis for further learning, in so natural a fashion that we are scarcely aware of being instructed.

The question of which psalms are suitable for teaching children depends on a number of factors. Personally, I am inclined to feel that the most important of these factors is that the psalms or psalm verses should be those for which the child finds a functional use. This in turn depends to some extent on the child's age and interests and on the amount of liturgical participation made possible by the home, the school and the parish church. Thus, by the time children are old enough to be taken to Mass with any regularity, it would seem most appropriate to teach them some of the psalms or verses that occur in the Mass.

■ *ORATE FRATRES, 1949*

PATRICK CUMMINS

1880–1968   Monk of Conception Abbey in Missouri; esteemed seminary professor for 48 years; rector at Sant' Anselmo College, 1920–1925; helped chart a course of integrating liturgy and life at Conception Abbey and Seminary; musician and composer; author and translator; one of the first associate editors of *Orate Fratres* and of the *American Benedictine Review*. He knew the *Divine Comedy* from memory in both Italian and English, translated it into English *terza rima* and taught to every young man who came to the monastery or seminary the poem's keystone, the line in Canto 17 that the choice of what and how one loves determines one's direction in life. His obituary noted: "Through his 68 years as a professed monk, he remained man among men, man of God, scholar, lover of wisdom, believer in people and in the day."

Importance of the homily during Mass

For Ambrose, Augustine, Chrysostom, Gregory, the spoken message was part and parcel of the Mass itself. Doctrine was elevated to matrimonial union with the eucharistic sacrifice and thus endowed with divine life. From the altar which is Christ, doctrine was stamped with the spirit of Christ and became, like Christ, perfect both in the divine order and in the human: perfect in the divine order, as theology; perfect in the human order, as literature.

What a contrast when we turn to modern Catholic speech! Oral instruction, the personal, local, concrete interpretation of the gospel message, is no longer the self-understood preparation for the holy sacrifice. Doctrine, once the fruitful spouse, who lived and moved in the sanctuary, has been sent forth from her home within that sanctuary, has been told to confine herself to the schoolroom, the platform, the lecture hall, even God save the mark!—to the printing office. Doctrine does indeed from time to time reappear in the holy place and reassume for the moment her rightful station. But even when she does thus reappear, on Sundays and feast days, she enters as a visitor, more or less welcome, no longer as mother and spouse.

■ *ORATE FRATRES, 1930*

Entrance song and procession

The intimate union between song and procession should make the action itself more effective. What are the effects to be expected from the processional singing of the Introit [entrance antiphon and psalm]? There are four:

A truer participation. A procession as such, at the beginning of the holy sacrifice, might appear as an external demonstration of solemnity and in our hands it might too often deteriorate into a vain parade. Even with the best intentions, we could hardly enter into the spirit of the eucharist just by walking along the precincts of the church, unless there is something to spur us on. The sacred melody called Introit takes hold of the procession, and while it is sung we are brought to realize that the clergy and the faithful are not marching but proceeding towards a momentous action, that of sharing Christ's sacrifice.

A deeper devotion. It is the power of song that it can move the soul; and, while it moves the soul of those who are proceeding to the altar, it prevents their falling into even a sincere formalism. If the procession is an external in the sacred liturgy, it shares through the song the values of an act of inner devotion. It is not the feet of the participants which the Introit leads to the eucharistic altar; it is their minds and their hearts that it wants to enkindle so that their whole being will be dedicated to Christ's celebration.

A dynamic piety. We all know that the eucharist is, of all religious experiences, the most dynamic, for there Christ reenacts his covenant of external love and of all-embracing redemption; then he consummates it by being to us, as it were, a living banquet. Does not the very character of the eucharist demand that we begin our participation in it with a dynamic introduction? Nothing will prompt such intense entrance but a procession with song, in which the movement of the body and the utterance of the voice join to arouse the soul towards an unlimited fervor.

Unity of all participants. To those who see in attending Mass nothing more than a personal privilege and an individual means of salvation, this last aspect will have no meaning. But to those who are aware that the eucharist, according to the authentic words of its institution, can be only the united offering of the whole church, the united singing of the Introit-processional will be a welcome incentive to celebrate the eucharist in the only way it can be properly celebrated; namely, in a corporate way.

■ *CAECILIA, 1944*

DOROTHY DAY

1897–1980   Convert to Catholicism; mother; cofounder
with Peter Maurin of *The Catholic Worker* newspaper and
House of Hospitality in New York, 1933; friend of Virgil
Michel; social and political activist from her early 20s until
her death. One of her aims was to bring the doctrine of the
Mystical Body to everyone. Under her guidance, the *Catholic
Worker* integrated concerns for liturgy and contemplation,
for the arts, for justice and peace and the embrace of poverty in Christian life. Of her the *Catholic Encyclopedia* says,
"For more than 50 years she led the most vital forces in this
'male-dominated' American church by enabling an experience of belief in the message of Jesus: 'The reign of God is in
your midst.'"

The power of the name

And now Cardinal Spellman, God bless him, has added still another prayer to those at the conclusion of Masses in the New York archdiocese, the Divine Praises: Blessed be God. Blessed be his holy name . . . and so on, like a creed, a declaration of faith. It is indeed an invocation of the name.

In regard to the name, Louis Bouyer in *The Meaning of Holy Scripture* has this to say: "It is the supreme expression of his presence (after the angel, the face, the Shekinah, his presence in the fire and the cloud) more spiritual and more personal than all the others."

Do we believe this, do we believe in the holy name and the power of the holy name? It was reading *The Way of the Pilgrim* that brought me first to a knowledge of what the holy name meant in our lives. Fordham Russian Center has a pamphlet, *On the Invocation of the Name,* which teaches us to pray without ceasing, with every breath we draw, with every beat of our hearts. And lastly, J. D. Salinger in the *New Yorker,* in his stories, *Frannie and Zooey,* later published in book form, brings us again to a concept of the meaning of the name.

With this recognition of the importance of the word made flesh and dwelling among us, still with us in the bread and wine of the altar, how can any priest tear through the Mass as though it were a repetitious duty? And some of the best priests I have met do this, abusing the prayers of the Mass in this way.

I am begging them not to.

"You cannot fail to see the power of mere words," Joseph Conrad wrote in his preface to *A Personal Record.* "Such words as glory, for instance, or pity. Shouted with perseverance, with ardor, with conviction, these two by their sound alone have set whole nations in motion and upheaved the dry hard ground on which rests our whole social fabric."

So I am praying that at the Council and at all the Masses at the Council, the word made flesh will be among them. Forsake them not, O Lord, our God.

■ *"On Pilgrimage,"* THE CATHOLIC WORKER, *c. 1960*

Compline at Catholic Worker

C harles (when he is not there, Ed takes over) gets through his hard job somehow. At last the crowd thins out with only a few loud talkers still sitting around. Joe Maurer, a late recruit who does just about everything around the place, starts handing out the Compline books. In a good strong voice, the product of Dominican vocal training, he leads us. (He also sings folk songs.) Soon we will drown out the talkers who have grown louder with the advancing hours. More than a dozen young people line up on either side of the clean, decorated dining room table. Joe leads one side, and Michael Kovalak, who was once in a Benedictine monastery and who also knows the psalm tones, leads the other.

"May the Lord Almighty grant us a peaceful night and a perfect end," says Joe.

"Amen," we all reply fervently.

"Be sober, be watchful," Michael on the other side warns in the words of St. Peter. "Your adversary the devil, as a roaring lion, goes about seeking someone to devour. Resist him, steadfast in the faith."

As we recite the Confiteor, I reflect that we, too, have sinned seventy times seven; and how much more than the seven times of the just man have we failed this very day! The absolution brings us the ease to go on with the psalms. The psalm for tonight is the 15th, and it touches my heart:

I set the Lord ever before me; with him at my right hand
I shall not be disturbed.
Therefore my heart is glad and my soul rejoices;
my body too abides in confidence;

because you will not abandon my soul to the nether world,
nor will you suffer your faithful one to undergo
 corruption.
You will show me the path to life,
fullness of joys in your presence,
delights at your right hand forever.

There is a hymn then, and the little chapter, and responsories and prayers.

Smokey Joe knows all these by heart—though he is not very tuneful. But then neither are the others. Some sing *basso profundo* and some sing *recto tono,* and if there is an Irish tenor he complicates the sound still more. It does not help matters that two or three older women who are tone deaf delight in singing too. But they enjoy themselves and it is the night prayer of the church, and God hears. The agnostic sings with the Catholic, because it is a communal act and he loves his brother. Our singing prepares us for another day. Early tomorrow morning the work will start again, and so our life, which St. Teresa of Avila described as a night spent in an uncomfortable inn, resumes. It will continue. The surroundings may be harsh, but where love is, God is.

■ *LOAVES AND FISHES, 1963*

Ordinary Time

The words "Ordinary Time" in our own prayer book put me in a state of confusion and irritation. To me, no times are "ordinary."

■ *"On Pilgrimage,"* THE CATHOLIC WORKER, *c. 1972*

Why go to Mass?

'm afraid that going to church puts many of us to sleep. We become so pleased with ourselves—our virtue, for attending Mass—that we forget about how others are living, who don't have the kind of lives we have. One of my non-Catholic friends once said to me, "Dorothy, Jesus never went to church on Sunday, so why do Catholics?" I thought he was being foolish and told him so. I explained the problem —the struggle Jesus had with some of the Jewish officials as well as the Roman ones. But my friend kept pushing me. "Jesus wanted people to love others, to give of themselves to others, not to fall in love with buildings and altars and prelates and popes, and not to give their time and money and faith to all that." I told him right, absolutely right. But he said I can't have it both ways, that I can't agree with him and with what "they" tell me in church. Well, I told him I can. I said I can go to church and pray to God, and when I pray, I can say anything I want, and God is listening, and no one else. Once I asked a priest in confession if I was being out of line by thinking thoughts like the one my friend had, while sitting there in church. He laughed and said he was afraid too many people don't have any thoughts in church; they just go through the motions. I told him I feel like crying sometimes, or I flush with anger: To be in church isn't to be calmed down, as some people say they get when they are at Mass. I'm worked up. I'm excited by being so close to Jesus, but the closer I get, the more I worry about what he wants of us, what he would have us do before we die.

■ *Interview with Robert Coles*

CATHERINE DE HUECK DOHERTY

1896–1985 Born in Russia; came to North America in 1921; founded Friendship House with her husband, Eddie, in Toronto, 1930; pioneer of the lay apostolate in Canada; founder and director of Madonna House, Combermere, Ontario; friend of Virgil Michel and of Godfrey Diekmann; author. She believed strongly in the link between liturgy and social action as attested in one of her letters: "I must confess I simply thought of it [liturgy] as the one and only way of feeding the little flock that the Lord had entrusted to me. For how else could dedication, zeal and service of our neighbor be fed, dispersed and grow?"

The eucharist and love for the poor

Eternally born anew in the stable, facing poverty, cold and hunger, spending his youth in narrow dirty streets between noisy trucks, overcrowded tenements, persecuted, forgotten, derided, abused, exploited, sold for thirty pieces of silver, neglected, beaten, spat upon and crucified over and over again, *Christ walks the earth in his poor.*

But there is worse. Those who have eyes can see his bloody face in the hearts of men and women, his body, bowed by the heavy cross, fall in exhaustion on the hard pavement of our streets. Oh, for thousands of Veronicas to wipe that holy face in the hearts of men and women!

And there is leprosy! Damien went to Molokai to nurse the leprous bodies of men and women. But what about the leprous souls? For sin disfigures our souls, and Christ within them, far worse than any disease can a body. A glance at a crucifix, a real one, is enough to know what sin has done to God! Oh, for thousands of Damiens, to nurse leprous souls to health and grace!

But where shall we get the courage to become other Veronicas and other Damiens? Love will give us this courage, love and faith. We can find both in the eucharist, where Christ lives with us unto the end of time. But we can do more, we can bring that love into our own hearts. We will find it in the liturgy of the church; daily Mass and daily communion will bring love from heaven into our sinful, weak hearts, and make them pure and strong with the strength of Christ, so that with St. Paul we shall be able to say: "I live now, not I, but Christ lives in me."

The daily sacrifice, fully participated in, will open to us the mind of Christ, and we will radiate him in our lives. And then we shall be able to go forth and fight the good fight of Christ against poverty, misery, injustice.

Participation in the Mass will teach us the full understanding of the Mystical Body of Christ, leading us to a Christian sociology, which is the cornerstone of the Christian social order and which alone can save our mad world from destruction.

In the liturgy we learn to know Christ. And if we truly know him, we shall recognize him everywhere, but especially in his poor, and we shall set our faces toward the liberation of him from the yoke of injustice and pain, helping to bring about the reign of Christ the King in this world. And with it order, peace and love, so that we shall be able to say: "I saw Christ today, and he was smiling."

■ *ORATE FRATRES, 1938*

ALCUIN DEUTSCH

1877–1951   Abbot of St. John's, Collegeville, 1921–1950; educated at Sant' Anselmo in Rome; encouraged the Liturgical Press and *Orate Fratres*. His weekly exhortations to the community often concerned walking in the presence of God, walking in faith.

Liturgy, the primary source

It seems to me that the hope for the renewal of the Christian life in our days lies in the active participation in the liturgy of the church. This is not my conviction only; that would carry little weight. I am echoing the mind of two illustrious vicars of Christ. Permit me to quote their words, even if they are not unfamiliar to you. Pius X wrote: "If the faithful were well instructed in the purpose desired by the church in instituting the sacred feasts and celebrated them in this spirit, there would be a notable renewal and increase of faith and piety, and consequently the interior life of the Christians would become much stronger and better." And Pius XI uttered the same conviction: "The annual celebration of the sacred mysteries is more efficacious for instructing the people in the matters of faith and thereby leading them to the interior joys of life than any, even the most weighty, pronouncements of the teaching church." And one of the foremost promoters of the so-called liturgical movement, Father Romano Guardini: "Those who come from the sacred realms of the liturgy to face their everyday problems will therein be able to radiate its force."

■ *Homily at the first National Liturgical Week, Chicago, 1940*

Total participation

Participation in the liturgy does not mean merely, or even principally, following the priest in the Mass by means of the missal, or responding to the prayers at Mass, or joining in the chant in congregational singing. All these things are merely external and material participation and may become merely mechanical, having no effect whatever in the promotion of spiritual union with Christ and renewal of our life in him. What is needed to have really fruitful participation unto practical Christian life is response to the love of Christ for us, which is brought before us in every Mass at which we assist, in every feast that we celebrate.

■ *Homily at the first National Liturgical Week, Chicago, 1940*

What we mean by "liturgy"

The first aim of the liturgical movement is to put the liturgy into our lives. Of this there can be no doubt. This is the import of the oft-quoted words of Pius X. He wanted the Christian spirit to flourish again among the faithful; he pointed out that the place where it is acquired is the Christian temple, that "its primary and indispensable source is the active participation in the most holy mysteries and in the public and solemn prayer of the church." In other words, he wanted active participation in the liturgy that thereby the Christian spirit might be generated and flourish in the hearts of the faithful and permeate their lives.

Let us note well what Pius X understands by the liturgy. It is not mere ritual: Active participation in it did not mean for him merely an explanation by the priest to the people of "ritual formulas and ceremonies," of "dogmatic and symbolical meanings and their historical origin," useful and necessary as this knowledge may be "for rendering the meaning of the Sunday, or the participation in the mysteries and other functions of the church properly intelligible, instructive, attractive, and fruitful." For Pius X the liturgy is "the most holy mysteries" and "the public and solemn prayer of the church": It is the sum total of the feasts which place before us the mysteries of God and Christ.

The liturgy was for the early Christians the expression of their devotion to Christ and therefore also the inspiration and guide of their life, which was in Christ and for Christ. Their worship modeled their life, and the *lex orandi* [rule of prayer] was for them not only the *lex credendi* [rule of faith] but also the *lex vivendi* [rule of life]. Such devotion to Christ and such a life in and for Christ is what Pius X meant by "active participation in the most holy mysteries and in the public and solemn prayer of the church." He meant that our soul should penetrate the mysteries of Christ and his church in a way that would make it vibrate with faith and love, love that would unite it with him, through the church as his Mystical Body, so as to lead a Christ life.

■ *Address to the priests of Buffalo, New York, 1927*

GODFREY DIEKMANN

1908– Monk of St. John's Abbey, Collegeville; studied at Sant' Anselmo and Maria Laach; retreat master; patristics scholar; renowned teacher; succeeded Virgil Michel as editor of *Orate Fratres/Worship* in 1938 and held that position for more than 25 years; one of the prime movers in the North American Liturgical Conference during the 1940s and 1950s and one of its most popular speakers; peritus at Vatican II; member of postconciliar Consilium for the implementation of liturgical reform; one of the founders of the International Commission on English in the Liturgy. Fred McManus once said of him: "His theological depth is equaled only by his charity. More than anyone else, he bridges the pastoral concerns and the spiritual, theological goals of liturgical change."

The interpretation of liturgical law

I would like particularly to speak as interpreting the mind of the late revered and beloved Dom Virgil Michel. First of all, a disciplinary pronouncement on liturgical law is not always inspired by the Holy Ghost, is not necessarily of itself the best expression of the true mind of the church; else, for example, the Holy Ghost must have reversed policy between the day before and the day after Pius X issued his famous decree on early and frequent holy communion.

The dogmatic theology of the church is of itself more fundamental and is the true approach to the mind of the church, but the normal external expression of that mind of the church is found in ecclesiastical laws, and hence it is not improper for those who have an adequate knowledge of theology to discuss and to criticize prudently current liturgical practices and laws. I say "prudently," for it is not desirable to arouse dissatisfaction that might (due to present conditions) come from altering a practice, without at the same time providing a positive and really spiritual, fitting and true outlook.

On the other hand, the law of the church is our law, and no greater harm can be done to the liturgical movement than, in the name of liturgy, to neglect or to disobey the law. The norms of the liturgy are fixed, and there's still much fundamental work to be done within the framework of that existing law, so even from this standpoint there is no reason to become too impatient with some of the recognized deficiencies of that framework. We still have a lot of work ahead of us to put life in the skeleton.

■ *Address at the first National Liturgical Week, Chicago, 1940*

Fed by God's word

St. Jerome wrote in language that is apt to startle us: "We eat Christ's flesh and drink his blood, not only in the sacrament [of the eucharist] but also in the reading of the scripture." Obviously his words cannot be taken literally, but the point he is making is clear: He is comparing the food of the eucharist and the spiritual food contained for us in the word of God. St. Augustine similarly says: "We are born spiritually, and we are constantly being spiritually born, through the word and the sacrament," the eucharist. As representative of the East, we might quote Origen, who had such a major influence on most of the great Eastern Fathers. He writes shortly after the year 200: "When the body of Christ is given you, you reverently and most carefully see to it that no crumb of it falls upon the ground. If, therefore, you employ such care, and rightly so, to preserve the body of Christ from profanation, how then can you think it a minor fault if you allow the word of God to go to waste?"

■ *Address at the Sisters' Institute of Spirituality, 1955*

Active participation: a recent history

Active participation has become something of a slogan and even the best slogan can easily be emptied by overuse. But that should not let us lose sight of the fact that almost all the great official papal directives in the last 50 years were designed to enlarge the scope of *participation* on the part of the members of the church. I repeat: In the last 50 years and more the popes have been urging the laity's active participation in *all* fields of Catholic life and effort.

It began most strikingly with Pope Leo XIII, the great social pope. He called for the active participation of the laity in bringing the Christian social message to the world. He asked every layperson to be a lay apostle in his or her own surroundings. He again made the Catholic layperson aware that he or she *had* an apostolate in the area of everyday life and work. Pope Leo XIII enlisted the help of the Catholic laity in order to restore Christ to the marketplace; to bring the principles of Christ inside the factory, into public life.

So far so good. But his successor, Pius X, went considerably further. In order to strengthen these lay apostles spiritually, he issued his demand that all the laity be granted active participation in the public worship of the church; for, as he said, such active participation is the chief and indispensable source of the true Christian spirit. He it was, too, who widened this participation to include frequent and even daily reception of holy communion. In a word: St. Pius X laid the profound spiritual foundations to the Christian apostolate outlined by Pope Leo XIII.

After St. Pius X came yet broader developments, and again, all of them were in terms of participation: the growing emphasis on the Mystical Body, clarifying the active role of the laity in the work of the church; the raising of Catholic action to significant official status; the encyclicals urging Bible reading by the laity; the change of the eucharistic fasting rules, to enable the faithful to receive communion more frequently; the introduction of evening Mass, again, for the sake of the laity; the extraordinarily significant restoration of the Easter Vigil, which, as our Holy Father explicitly tells us, was done precisely in order to make possible a better understanding and a greater degree of participation by the faithful; and only last year, we American Catholics received the generous gift of our mother tongue in a number of the sacraments and sacramentals. Again, for what other purpose than to allow the laity to take a more active and intelligent part in the sacred rites?

■ *Catholic Hour radio address, 1955*

The paschal mystery

The Mass is the memorial of Christ's death *and* resurrection. Such has been the faith of the church from the very outset. This explains the fact that Sunday, that is to say, the day of his resurrection, was chosen as the day on which to celebrate the holy eucharist. It explains too why Easter was the first feast to be specially observed and to be celebrated by means of holy Mass. This conviction, of holy Mass being the memorial of resurrection as well as death, found literary expression in the very first text that has come down to us, of what we would now call the canon: It is found in the *Apostolic Tradition* of St. Hippolytus of Rome, written about the year 215. Paul, writing of the eucharistic celebration, said: "For as often as you shall eat this bread and drink this cup, you proclaim the death of the Lord, until he comes" (1 Corinthians 11:26). And quoting Jesus' words: "This is my body which shall be given up for you; do this in remembrance of me" (1 Corinthians 11:24). He himself refers directly only to his saving death. And yet, the church, certainly as early as St. Hippolytus and to our own day, immediately after quoting Christ's words, "Do this in remembrance of me," infallibly interprets these words for us: "Wherefore, mindful *not only* of his blessed passion *but also of his resurrection* from the grave offer unto thy majesty. . . ."

■ *Address at the National Liturgical Week, Cincinnati, 1958*

The dynamism of the eucharist

The eucharist is not something static. The gift becomes the obligation. The eucharist is something dynamic, a life that demands to be lived. We receive Christ for a purpose, not to keep him for ourselves but to give him to others so that they may recognize him in us.

■ *THEOLOGY DIGEST, 1962*

The depth of change and the need for instruction

The most important objective is to plan and effect systematic instruction of the people, not just in *practice* but in *reorientation* of our whole spiritual life. This is not the change contemplated by the liturgical movement or the earlier schema. It is a question of orientating our whole spiritual life, of rethinking things in terms of Christ, the church and our role in the church. This is therefore a lifelong program and we can never instruct sufficiently. Nevertheless this instruction must begin immediately or we'll have spiritual activism, as Paul says, "a tinkling cymbal." If the liturgical movement is not basically a spiritual movement, it is nothing, and that means a constant instruction and learning by doing, but the two must go hand in hand. But of the two, learning is more basic, not only for laity but for priests. Priests must be willing to read, to study, to find underlying motives for reform. Unless they realize that these things flow from the very nature of the church, they will not be sufficiently personally involved to make this matter one to which they devote themselves with all their heart.

■ *Interview in Rome, 1963*

The problem of large parishes

Plato recognized that community ceases where personal relationships become impossible. The structuring of the people of God into mammoth congregations instead of communities would seem to be the greatest long-range pastoral, and therefore liturgical, problem facing the American church. At the Council, in the discussion of the role of bishops, the schema enunciated as a first principle that a diocese normally be only so large that the bishop can personally know his priests. What a structural revolution would ensue if this principle were to be applied further to the parish! Is the phenomenal success of the Cursillo movement in our day due perhaps to the fact that these people are, for the first time in their lives, experiencing that sense of Christian community which the eucharistic assembly and celebration gave to Christians of early times, and are of their nature meant to give today? We know that various palliative expedients are being tried; for example, weekday Masses in homes. Historically, parishes developed from dioceses solely in order to insure the possibility of personal pastor-to-people and people-to-people relationships. Whatever the difficulties, and they are mountainous, it would seem imperative therefore that our superparishes similarly undergo a new structuring into community-sized groupings. For only thus can the divine command, reiterated by Trent, be observed: that the pastor know his flock by name, that is, as persons. Only thus can eucharist make a true people of God.

■ *Address at the National Liturgical Week, Chicago, 1965*

Baptism's rights and duties

I am one of those who believe that Vatican Council II, despite all the publicity attached to the indubitably important matter of collegiality of bishops and their role and authority vis-à-vis the Holy See, will most radically affect the future policy and life of the church by its honest effort to restore full responsible citizenship to the laity. The church, St. Paul reminds us, is founded "on the apostles *and prophets*, with Christ himself the chief cornerstone" (Ephesians 2:20). The liturgy, as the *Constitution on the Sacred Liturgy* states, is both summit and source of the Church's activity and power (10). "Full, conscious and active participation in it by the Christian people is their right and duty by reason of their baptism" (14). It is the root that demands and makes possible flowering in apostolic work. Not the sacrament of holy orders, as the recent 1958 Instruction of the Congregation of Rites still presupposed when it spoke of commentators, readers and choir members having a "delegated" ministry, but the sacraments of baptism and confirmation that confer full worshiping and teaching and ruling rights according to rank in "the chosen race, the royal priesthood" (1 Peter 2:9). It is significant that this passage from 1 Peter is one of the most frequently quoted scripture texts in the conciliar documents—and all of them, in treating of the laity's role, invariably call attention to its baptismal, liturgical foundation. The clericalization of the church, the most injurious imbalance reaching back certainly to the sixth century, by which an ecclesiology had become a hierarchology, had found its first expression in liturgical worship. It was therefore appropriate that in liturgical action and theory it be first and most radically abolished.

It can only be regretted, however, that this active role of the laity, so urgently proclaimed by the liturgy constitution in theory, was completely overlooked in practice in the composition of the document which was chiefly for their benefit. No layperson, so far as I know, was directly asked to give advice. Certainly none was part of the preparatory liturgical commission or the commission that functioned during the Council. This, I believe, is the most flagrant flaw of the *Constitution:* A house was built without consulting the persons who are to live in it. As to that, I further believe that the commissions would have been significantly aided in their work had they enlisted the collaboration of competent spokespersons of the worship traditions of other Christian communities, not only of the so-called liturgical churches, those of Anglicans and Lutherans, but also of the evangelical and free Churches. The Quakers, for instance, would have valuable advice for us about the community-formative power of silence.

■ *Address at the University of Notre Dame, 1966*

Dangers in reform

U nless and until the theology of the liturgy is accepted
and ever more fully understood, the so-called practical
liturgical reforms will necessarily fail of their intended effect.
They will be little more than a transition from a previous
state of passivity to one of a new ritual formalism.

And I have a desperate fear that our American liturgical
movement in all too many parishes and dioceses has, since
the Council and the introduction of the reforms, fallen victim to this changed but more virulent form of ritualism.
Shifting about furniture, for instance, without even knowing
or caring why it is being shifted, is scarcely a guaranteed
way of initiating a new Pentecost. It is not an accident that
immediately after stating its theology of the liturgy, the *Constitution,* in articles 14–20, urgently insists on liturgical
instruction, formation, and even promotes the study of the
liturgy in seminaries to the rank of a major course. I believe
there can be no doubt whatever that in the mind of the
Council these articles on the need of constant and patient
and thorough instruction on the theology and spirit of the
liturgy follow in immediate importance the theological statement itself and have clear priority over all the succeeding
practical directives of reform.

■ *"The Theology of Liturgy According to Vatican II," 1967*

Worshiping worthily

Q uite frankly, I am no longer able to find any valid
meaning in our customary clichés about a church
building or religious art or music or liturgical ritual that is
"worthy of God." The phrase can have significance, it seems
to me, not in terms of any *thing,* of any *it,* but only on the
basis of whether or not that thing or object or rite is a suitable means for the transformation of men and women in

their Christian task of loving neighbor and of loving and worthily serving God. Yet how long we have been preoccupied with the beauty of the church edifice, the beauty of ceremonial, the beauty of music, which is worthy of God, instead of asking ourselves first of all: What can best move these persons' faith, what can move their will to love? What else can be truly worthy of God except *persons* who believe more fully, who love God and their neighbor more deeply and learn to do so in the Mass?

■ *WORSHIP, 1967*

GREGORY DIX

1901–1952   Monk of the Anglican abbey of Nashdom; author and lecturer. Dix was the first to demonstrate that the classic fourfold shape of the eucharist (the preparation, the prayer of praise and thanksgiving, the fraction rite, and communion) is modeled on the pattern of the institution narratives in the synoptic gospels. His classic work, *The Shape of the Liturgy,* has been reprinted many times since its original publication in 1945.

Anamnesis

D o this in memory of me." Was ever another command
so obeyed? For century after century, spreading slowly
to every continent and country and among every race on
earth, this action has been done, in every conceivable human
circumstance, for every conceivable human need from
infancy and before it to extreme old age and after it, from
the pinnacles of earthly greatness to the refuge of fugitives in
the caves and dens of the earth. We have found no better
thing than this to do for kings at their crowning and for
criminals going to the scaffold; for armies in triumph or for
a bride and bridegroom in a little country church; for the
proclamation of a dogma or for a good crop of wheat; for
the wisdom of the Parliament of a mighty nation or for a
sick old woman afraid to die; for a schoolboy sitting an
examination or for Columbus setting out to discover America; for the famine of whole provinces or for the soul of a
dead lover; in thankfulness because my father did not die of
pneumonia; for a village headman much tempted to return
to fetish because the yams had failed; because the Turk was
at the gates of Vienna; for the repentance of Margaret; for
the settlement of a strike; for a child for a barren woman;
for Captain so-and-so, wounded and prisoner of war; while
the lions roared in the nearby amphitheatre; on the beach at
Dunkirk; while the hiss of scythes in the thick June grass
came faintly through the windows of the church; trem-
ulously, by an old monk on the 50th anniversary of his
vows; furtively by an exiled bishop who had hewn timber all
day in a prison camp near Murmansk; gorgeously, for the
canonization of St. Joan of Arc—one could fill many pages
with the reasons why we have done this and not tell a hun-
dredth part of them. And best of all, week by week and
month by month, on a hundred thousand successive Sundays, faithfully, unfailingly, across all the parishes of

Christendom, the pastors have done this just to *make* the
plebs sancta Dei—the holy common people of God.

■ *THE SHAPE OF THE LITURGY, 1945*

Liturgy as the pattern for a lifetime

To those who know a little of Christian history, probably
the most moving of all the reflections it brings is not the
thought of great events and the well-remembered saints but
of those innumerable millions of entirely obscure faithful
men and women, every one with his or her own individual
hopes and fears and joys and sorrows and loves—and sins
and temptations and prayers—once every whit as vivid and
alive as mine are now. They have left no slightest trace in this
world, not even a name, but have passed to God utterly forgotten. Yet each of them once believed and prayed as you
and I believe and pray, and found it hard and grew slack and
sinned and repented and fell again. Each of them worshiped
with others, and found their thoughts wandering and tried
again and again, and felt heavy at the eucharist and unre-
sponsive and yet knew—just as really and pathetically as I
do these things. There is a little ill-spelled ill-carved rustic
epitaph of the fourth century from Asia Minor:—"Here
sleeps the blessed Chione, who has found Jerusalem for she
prayed much." Not another word is known of Chione, some
peasant woman who lived in that vanished world of Christian Anatolia. But how lovely if all that should survive after
16 centuries were that one had prayed, so that the neighbors
who saw all one's life were sure one must have found Jerusalem! What did the Sunday eucharist in her village church
every week for a lifetime mean to the blessed Chione—and to
the millions like her then, and every year since? The sheer stupendous *quantity* of the love of God which this ever repeated
action has drawn from the obscure Christian multitudes
through the centuries is in itself an overwhelming thought.

■ *THE SHAPE OF THE LITURGY, 1945*

MICHAEL DUCEY

1897–1970   Monk of St. Benedict's Abbey, Benet Lake, Wisconsin; later of St. Anselm's Priory in Washington, D.C.; chief organizer of the first National Liturgical Week in Chicago, 1940; for years served the Liturgical Conference in various offices and behind the scenes. He dreamed of founding a monastery whose primary work would be the promotion of the liturgical apostolate in the United States.

The liturgy and time

When we come to examine the origin and structure of the liturgical year, which cannot properly be understood unless in direct relation with the eucharistic sacrifice, for which it provides a marvelously beautiful, ideally arranged external setting, we find that it represents the sum total of the church's effort to sanctify time, to dedicate every possible moment of its passage, as it were, to the service of God and the celebration of the mysteries of redemption. Thus, the Sunday, the weekdays, the four seasons of the year, certain hours of the day and night, the anniversaries of the martyrs, all received at a very early date a special place in liturgical worship. The vigils, the day hours, ember days, station days, Lent and Advent, Holy Week, became familiar accompaniments to the eucharistic sacrifice, almost as soon as the Christians were able to organize their communal assemblies. And although the raw material, as it were, out of which they were hewn, was supplied by current temporal observances among the Jews and Romans, the Christians gave them an entirely new significance, a unique, absolutely original character, in keeping with the august mystery which they served to adorn. It was, in brief, that same deep spiritual *enthusiasm* which we saw reflected from the very first beginnings of eucharistic worship: a deep-seated faith and confidence in the risen Christ, joy and gratitude over the blessings of redemption, eager anticipation of his coming, sincerest mutual love and fellowship. And like the ceremonies of the Mass, these methods of designating the temporal circumstances of its offering became finally fixed, officially determined by the church by the onset of the Middle Ages.

■ *Address at the National Liturgical Week, Portland, 1947*

Finally, silence and few words and hope

Faith must be uppermost in all our approaches to liturgy. Our efforts to understand the Mass better, and to expand our knowledge of the rich doctrinal content of the liturgical year, are indeed praiseworthy, eminently useful. But in making them, we must never forget that ultimately we shall reach a point beyond which our mere human intellects cannot go. For here we are faced with the great central *mystery* of our Catholic adoration, and the mind ceases its restless searchings, giving way to the mysterious promptings of the Holy Spirit. Indeed, it is this lesson above all, I think, that is taught us by the early Christians, as they formed and fashioned the external framework of our worship with such consummate skill; namely, that here, as we are plunged into the very depths of Christ's redeeming act, with all its stupendous implications, we must at length be content to rest in adoring silence, or at best, to utter only words of joyous, reverent homage and thanksgiving; and finally to await, confident in our hope, for that great day when the enshrouding veils of mystery shall be torn away, giving place to the resplendent glory of the beatific vision.

■ *Address at the National Liturgical Week, Portland, 1947*

BENEDICT EHMANN

1906– Benedictine monk; ordained 1929; apostle of the liturgy; capable musician. He had the gift of fine literary expression and was editor of *Catholic Choirmaster.*

Communal life of the church

B esides being functional and sacramental, the Christ-life of the church is social, what I would rather call communal. I would call it communist except somebody else has preempted that word. The true religion is not a matter of mere private converse with God, segregated from the religion of one's fellows. In the body of Christ, membership demands coordination and cooperation. We must allow a true value, of course, to inner devotional life: but that inner communing of the spirit with its God must draw its meaning and energy from the communion of saints which is incorporation into Christ. The communal life of the church depends upon inner asceticism and devotion to protect it from formalism and routine; on the other hand, personal devotion demands communion with the Mystical Body of Christ, if it is not to become artificial and anemic.

■ *Address at the first National Liturgical Week, Chicago, 1940*

The meaning of piety

P iety is family spirit. The children growing up within the family circle receive a thousand influences which profoundly and subtly mold their character and direct their loyalties. Its traditions and memories become theirs and are transmitted to the future through them. In its soil their roots strike deep, and in its light and warmth their branches grow and come to the time of fruitfulness. The ensemble of their family love, family reverence, family loyalty, family spirit, may be comprised in the single word "piety."

This larger notion of the word "piety" needs to be insisted upon for the people of our time, for whom so many words have been degraded into inane and insipid meanings. Piety is not a sickly emotion for weaklings who live in a dream world of their own. Piety is a virtue as strong and as imperious as the blood in our veins. It is family spirit.

■ *Address at the National Liturgical Week, New York, 1944*

The alphabet of God's meaning

We are human, and we move slowly, like dull pupils laboring at the alphabet of God's meaning. This "putting on of Christ," which is the essence of Christian piety, is no quick or easy matter. For it we need the church, not only as the dispenser of the Christ-life, but also as our teacher and counselor in it. And the church, under the inspiration of the Holy Spirit, has devised a most simple and wise way for the following of Christ. It is a way that is truest to life, for it lives what it teaches and teaches while it lives. It is the way of the liturgical year, evolved slowly through the centuries and maturing into a form which is the most potent instrument of supernatural pedagogy in the world. In comparison with it, all spiritual exercises and methods of piety are but secondary auxiliaries.

■ *Address at the National Liturgical Week, New York, 1944*

GERALD ELLARD

1894–1963   Jesuit priest; professor of liturgy at St. Mary's College in Kansas for 30 years; one of the founders and a steady contributor to *Orate Fratres/Worship;* his writings include *Christian Life and Worship,* the finest college text for many years; first version of the American ritual was largely his work; author of pamphlets for the Popular Liturgical Library; frequent speaker at National Liturgical Weeks. He decided early in life to dedicate his work to popular education in liturgy. Though he did not mingle easily and some found him hard to get to know, those who did know him called him "a gentle scholar, a man of practical understanding as well as deep piety." At his death *Worship* gave him the following tribute: "To some, he was a little known priest of the Society of Jesus; to some an intimate friend and counselor. To many he was a kind and gentle human being marked by his mildness and meekness. Some knew him as a scholar; [some knew him] from the gentle humor of the classroom or the retreat conference. To many he was a symbol — a symbol of liturgical life and growth."

Social sanctification in baptism and eucharist

How is liturgy social sanctification? It will help us to picture the social sanctification of the sacramental system if we make a swift survey. Given the elemental necessity and importance of baptism, it is a divinely generous provision that anyone at all may baptize. But still no one may baptize himself or herself: The very nature of the rite demands self-surrender to God expressed by self-surrender to another human being, who affords social assistance.

Of the greatest of all the sacraments, and the Christian sacrifice, the holy eucharist, we constrain ourselves to bring forward but one single brief quotation from him whom we now call Cardinal Stritch: "The holy eucharist among the Christian sacraments," he said, "is *par excellence* a great social sacrament, the symbol of true social unity in the Mystical Body of Christ and the pledge of that unity to all people of good will. The sacrifice of the Mass is a great social act. It is the prayer and the sermon of the Mystical Body of Christ. The eucharist is the source of this social unity in Christ's plan. It is the food which nourishes, invigorates, and preserves the life of the church, Christ's Mystical Body, his basic social plan."

The Catholic church has been described as "those who love Christ, and for love of him love one another." Good as the test is, it is not as clear cut as Christ's own statement: "The mark by which all will know you for my disciples will be the love you bear one another" (John 13:35). "Christ's basic social plan," the Cardinal says. Social worship, we have seen, begets social thinking and acting, flowers into Christian fellowship, brings out the Christ in us. That is why in 1937 Cardinal Rodrique Villeneuve, Archbishop of Quebec, gave it as his measured judgment: "In our day, when every effort is being made to instill a religious spirit into society, it would be a lamentable mistake to give a predominant place, above liturgy, to various organizations and pious works, whose supernatural efficacy depends entirely on how much they are imbued with a liturgical sense. And therefore, among the many activities of Catholic action, the liturgical apostolate should be given the first place."

■ *Address at the National Liturgical Week, Denver, 1946*

Perfect profession of love

Let the Mass be described as the perfect profession of love. Thus: "On Sundays the perfect profession of love is offered in this church at seven and eight and half-past nine, eleven and twelve-fifteen o'clock, and on week-days, at six-thirty, seven-thirty and eight-thirty."

The perfect profession of love, the profession of perfect love, love's surest test offered before all, love's fairest flower caught and held, love's whitest ardor burning bright, love's deepest passion, God-like love. Love itself has its instinctive language the whole world over from infancy to second childhood, and from one end of the cultural scale to the other, all peoples know the language of love, or rather, I should say, the languages of love, for love speaks *three* languages: It begins with *words;* it goes on to *giving presents;* and perfect love will *culminate in service.*

The most elemental thing about love is that it refuses to be silent: It *will* declare itself, and it will *find* the way, the *best* way to disclose its message. The readiest medium, of course, is speech, and lovers exhaust the resources of the dictionary in trying to find words capable of embodying the full reality of their love. But love is never satisfied that words can do it justice and feels that there must be a natural sign-language more expressive here than words. So, in the second stage, so to say, love turns to giving gifts, feeling the present is the love embodied, the love made tangible, transferable. Even the baby in arms will pick a frayed thread from mamma's dress and give it to her with a smile; and I dare say that even in a baby-way it knows that the frayed thread has no special value by itself, but given with a smile it becomes a vessel full of love. Growing love struggles ever with the problem of finding the best gift, the most eloquent gift, the least unsatisfactory gift as it in turn tries "saying it" with candy, with flowers, with jewelry, all of which have their own appropriateness, all of which have their own limitations in voicing the full message of perfect love.

If this love be such that lovers are ready to put the whole of their future at the feet of the beloved, what, then, is the symbol of their choice? Do they not go to the jewelry store and purchase a diamond ring, something exquisitely precious in its own right, but a thousand times more so by reason of the *lifelong service* which it pledges? And when preliminary promise is later fulfilled, is not the wedding ring the traditional pledge of a life of service for one another? Is it only the love of husband and wife that has such symbolic expression? Is not the nun's veil a similar pledge of selfless love dedicated to fullest service? Is not the monk's scapular a similar sign to the world that love has led him to make of his life a lasting holocaust of service? Is not the priest's collar a similar token of love's yoke freely assumed, joyously borne, honorably professed? In religion or out of it, the human heart can voice its love in words, in gifts, and in service: That is the finest gift, which, given with suitable words, betokens lifelong service. That is the fullest love that lives up to its pledges.

■ *Address at the National Liturgical Week, Portland, 1947*

ROMANO GUARDINI

1885–1968   Born in Verona, Italy, but spent his life in Germany; a leader in European thought during three generations; discovered the centrality of the liturgy through contact with the Benedictines of Beuron, then at Maria Laach; ministered to German youth, then became a member of the Catholic theological faculty at the University of Bonn. He had frail health, and suffered from severe depression, yet he believed this suffering enabled him to develop both depth and stability. His works, including *The Spirit of the Liturgy, The Church and the Catholic,* and *Liturgical Education,* had a great effect on the liturgical movement.

The sign of the cross

When we cross ourselves, let it be with a real sign of the cross. Instead of a small cramped gesture that gives no notion of its meaning, let us make a large unhurried sign, from forehead to breast, from shoulder to shoulder, consciously feeling how it includes the whole of us, our thoughts, our attitudes, our body and soul, every part of us at once, how it consecrates and sanctifies us.

It does so because it is the sign of the universe and the sign of our redemption. On the cross Christ redeemed humankind. By the cross he sanctifies us to the last shred and fiber of our being. We make the sign of the cross before we pray to collect and compose ourselves and to fix our minds and hearts and wills upon God. We make it when we finish praying in order that we may hold fast the gift we have received from God. In temptations we sign ourselves to be strengthened; in dangers, to be protected. The cross is signed upon us in blessings in order that the fullness of God's life may flow into the soul and fructify and sanctify us wholly.

Think of these things when you make the sign of the cross. It is the holiest of all signs. Make a large cross, taking time, thinking what you do. Let it take in your whole being —body, soul, mind, will, thoughts, feelings, your doing and not-doing—and by signing yourself with the cross strengthen and consecrate the whole in the strength of Christ, in the name of the triune God.

■ *SACRED SIGNS, 1927*

Kneeling

When does our littleness so come home to us as when we stand in God's presence? God is the great God who is today and yesterday, whose years are hundreds and thousands, who fills the place where we are, the city, the wide world, the measureless space of the starry sky, in whose eyes the universe is less than a particle of dust, all-holy, all-pure, all-righteous, infinitely high. God is so great, I so small, so small that beside God I seem hardly to exist, so wanting am I in worth and substance. One has no need to be told that God's presence is not the place in which to stand on one's dignity. To appear less presumptuous, to be as little and low as we feel, we sink to our knees and thus sacrifice half our height; and to satisfy our hearts still further, we bow down our heads; and our diminished stature speaks to God and says: Thou art the great God; I am nothing. Therefore let not the bending of our knees be a hurried gesture, an empty form. Put meaning into it. To kneel, in the soul's intention, is to bow down before God in deepest reverence.

■ *SACRED SIGNS, 1927*

Bread and wine

Bread is food. It is wholesome, nourishing food for which we never lose our appetite. Under the form of bread God becomes for us even the food of life. "We break a bread," writes St. Ignatius of Antioch to the faithful at Ephesus, "we break a bread that is the food of immortality." By this food our being is so nourished with God that we exist in God and God in us.

Wine is drink. To be exact, it is more than drink, more than a liquid like water that merely quenches thirst. "Wine that makes glad the heart of man and woman" is the biblical expression. The purpose of wine is not only to quench thirst but also to give pleasure and satisfaction and exhilaration. "My cup, how good it is, how plenteous!" Literally, how intoxicating, though not in the sense of drinking to excess. Wine possesses a sparkle, a perfume, a vigor, that expands and clears the imagination. Under the form of wine Christ gives us his divine blood. It is no plain and sober draught. It was bought at a great price, at a divinely excessive price. Blood of Christ, inebriate me, prays St. Ignatius, that knight of the burning heart. In one of the antiphons for the feast of St. Agnes, the blood of Christ is called a mystery of ineffable beauty. "I have drawn milk and honey from his lips, and his blood hath given fair color to my cheeks."

For our sakes Christ became bread and wine, food and drink. We make bold to eat him and to drink him. This bread gives us solid and substantial strength. This wine bestows courage, joy out of all earthly measure, sweetness, beauty, limitless enlargement and perception. It brings life in intoxicating excess, both to possess and to impart.

■ *SACRED SIGNS, 1927*

Standing

The respect we owe to the infinite God requires of us a bearing suited to such a presence. The sense that we have of the greatness of God's being and, in God's eyes, of the slightness of our own is shown outwardly by our kneeling down to make ourselves small. But reverence has another way of expressing itself. When you are sitting down to rest or chat and someone to whom you owe respect comes in and turns to speak to you, at once you stand up and remain standing so long as he or she is speaking and you are answering. Why do we do this?

In the first place to stand up means that we are in possession of ourselves. Instead of sitting relaxed and at ease, we take hold of ourselves; we stand, as it were, at attention, geared and ready for action. Persons on their feet can come or go at once. They can take an order on the instant or carry out an assignment the moment they are shown what it is that is wanted.

Standing is the other side of reverence toward God. Kneeling is the side of worship in rest and quietness; standing is the side of vigilance and action. It is the respect of the servant in attendance, of the soldier on duty.

When the good news of the gospel is proclaimed, we stand up. Godparents stand when in the child's place they make the solemn profession of faith, children when they renew these promises at their first communion. Bridegroom and bride stand when they bind themselves at the altar to be faithful to their marriage vow. On these and the like occasions we stand up.

Even when we are praying alone, to pray standing may more forcibly express our inward state. The early Christians stood by preference. The *orante,* in the familiar catacomb representation, stands in the long flowing robes of a woman of rank and prays with outstretched hands, in perfect freedom, perfect obedience, quietly attending to the word and in readiness to perform it with joy.

We may feel at times a sort of constraint in kneeling. One feels freer standing up, and in that case standing is the right position. But stand up straight: not leaning, both feet on the ground, the knees firm, not slackly bent, upright, in control. Prayer made thus is both free and obedient, both reverent and serviceable.

■ *SACRED SIGNS, 1927*

Does liturgy have a purpose?

G rave and earnest people who seek for a definite purpose everywhere tend to experience a peculiar
difficulty where the liturgy is concerned. They incline to
regard it as being to a certain extent aimless, as superfluous
pageantry of a needlessly complicated and artificial character. What is the use of it all? The essential part of eucharist—
the action of sacrifice and the divine banquet—could be so
easily consummated. Why, then, the need for the solemn
institution of the priestly office? The necessary consecration
could be so simply accomplished in so few words, and the
sacraments so straightforwardly administered—what is the
reason for all the prayers and ceremonies? The liturgy tends
to strike people of this turn of mind as—to use the words
which are really most appropriate—trifling and theatrical.
The question is a serious one. It does not occur to everyone,
but in the people whom it does affect it is a sign of the mental attitude which concentrates on and pursues that which is
essential. It appears to be principally connected with the
question of purpose.

The liturgy has laid down the serious rules of the sacred
game which the soul plays before God. And, if we are
desirous of touching bottom in this mystery, it is the Spirit of
fire and of holy discipline "who has knowledge of the word"
—the Holy Spirit—who ordained the game which the eternal wisdom plays before God in the church, its kingdom on
earth. And "its delight" is in this way "to be with the children of men and women."

Only those not scandalized by this understand what the
liturgy means. From the very first every type of rationalism
has turned against it. The practice of the liturgy means that
by the help of grace, under the guidance of the church, we
grow into living works of art before God, with no other aim
or purpose than that of living and existing in God's sight; it

means fulfilling God's word and "becoming as *little children*"; it means forgoing maturity with all its purposefulness and confining oneself to play, as David did when he danced before the ark. It may, of course, happen that those extremely clever people, who merely from being grown-up have lost all spiritual youth and spontaneity, will misunderstand this and jibe at it. David probably had to face the derision of Michal.

It is in this very aspect of the liturgy that its didactic aim is to be found, that of teaching the soul not to see purposes everywhere, not to be too conscious of the end it wishes to attain, not to be desirous of being overly clever and grown-up, but to understand simplicity in life. The soul must learn to abandon, at least in prayer, the restlessness of *purposeful activity;* it must learn to *waste time* for the sake of God and to be prepared for the sacred game with sayings and thoughts and gestures, without always immediately asking "why?" and "wherefore?" It must learn not to be continually yearning to *do* something, to attack something, to accomplish something useful, but to play the divinely ordained game of the liturgy in liberty and beauty and holy joy before God.

■ *THE SPIRIT OF THE LITURGY, 1931*

PAUL HALLINAN

1911–1968   Bishop of Charleston, then archbishop of
Atlanta; champion of the liturgical reform who integrated it
with strong ecclesial and social concerns; ecumenist; leader
in questions of interracial justice; chairman of the Bishops'
Committee on the Liturgy; the only American bishop on the
conciliar commission on the liturgy at which appointment he
is reported to have said he was "surprised, delighted, and
scared"; cofounder of the International Commission on
English in the Liturgy; member of the Consilium after Vatican II. Of him it was said, "There was no problem of a
credibility gap; what he said he meant, and one could count
on his loyalty."

Liturgical renewal and courtesy

Zeal we need for liturgical renewal, but we also need tact and courtesy and kindness and persuasion, and all these are the ways of charity. The law of love has not been repealed by the new *Constitution*. The foremost mark of those who love the liturgy should be a deep humility. Most of us can confess quite easily, "There but for the grace of God and *Mediator Dei*—go I!"

■ *Address at the National Liturgical Week, St. Louis, 1964*

The liturgy is for the people

It is the people, God's holy people, that make up the church, that *need* the liturgy. For the liturgy is not created nor made up by the church. It is received from God, but it can exist only for the people. It will be helpful for us to examine this. There will be changes in it—English for Latin in some places, certain other changes, more scripture. But the chief transformation will not be on the surface but rather in the fundamental things: the effect on *you personally*, on the *parish*, on the *church* and on those *separated from the church* but still joined by baptism.

You are asked to come out from behind the pillar and put away your rosary. You are *asked to join with the priest in a community prayer and action*, first drawing in the riches of the Bible, then participating in the eucharist, particularly by receiving Christ's body and blood. Your prayers, hymns, responses and gestures will be important. All the while, you will be more conscious of yourself, your family, your neighbor as part of this "holy people." Through the priest, who is Christ's representative, you are taking your part in the Mystical Body.

■ *Pastoral letter in 1964*

The freedom to create

Given our flair for the novel, an authentic liturgy needs order, norms and competent authority. Few would opt for an anarchy of the altar. But given any institution's built-in centripetal force, the leaders of the liturgy must find the time to experiment, to change, to adapt—in a word, to create. The last thing the renewal needs is a liturgical Pentagon.

■ *Address at the National Liturgical Week, Milwaukee, 1967*

On liturgical collaboration

If we ever needed liturgical teamwork, mutual trust, pooled energies and skills, it is right now. Out of it could emerge a true unity, not imposed from above or forced from below, but a unity in which every part of the church could give its best to the eucharist, the word and the sacraments. There must come about a mutual trust in which bishops declare a moratorium on their angry repressions and condemnations and priests stop thinking of their bishops as the authoritarian baron-bishops of the ninth and tenth centuries. As we work together, forgetting our prejudices and curbing our self-will, we can serve our people not from the top of a pyramid of power, but in your midst where we can hear you and heed you.

■ *Address at a regional liturgical conference, 1967*

The American context of liturgical renewal

As members of the American church, we cannot allow ourselves to be deceived by a distorted view of tradition, for two of the discernible characteristics of American Catholicism are its brevity (we are less than 200 years old) and its immigrant origin. This is the hour, this is the day when we must find our identity as a people whose worship flows from their very life—a life that has been both enriched and emasculated by the dissolution of our ethnic ghettos, by the mobility of our population, by the inauguration of a computerized technology, by the environment that is saturated with gadgets and an overpowering media, and lastly, by an affluence that can be used for the service of humankind or that can isolate us from the cries of our brothers and sisters all over the world.

Within the present framework of our church, there is no opportunity as great as the repetitive assembling of men and women to engage in that work which we call liturgy. We—members of a nation whose identity has been forged from the anvil of the unknown, and who politically have sought a league of nations, a new deal, a new frontier and a great society—cannot be afraid of experimentation within the confines of the ecclesiastical. This experimentation is rooted in the concept of radical adaptation, an adaptation that has taken place in our liturgy as it went from the upper room and the paschal meal, the *eucharistia* of the *Didache*, the Leonine, Gelasian and Gregorian sacramentaries, the Romano-Frankish Mass of the tenth century to the missal of Pius v.

We are now emerging from a period of fixity and rigidity which was unnatural in the church's life. The *Constitution on the Sacred Liturgy*, as are so many other documents of the Council, is not a completed blueprint to construct the edifice of a new liturgy. The *Constitution* is a declaration of principle with practical norms and a style of its own. If we evaluate it solely in juridical terms, it will share the same fate as the decrees of the Council of Trent, "which the theologians considered for several centuries as the complete epitome of the whole tradition of the church." We must understand that this declaration of principle must be applied and adapted, tested and evaluated with a healthy respect for anthropology as well as theology.

■ *A month before his death, 1968*

MARTIN B. HELLRIEGEL

1891–1981 Pastor of Holy Cross Parish, St. Louis, Missouri, for 40 years and made it a model of pastoral liturgical practice; for 22 years was chaplain to the Precious Blood Sisters of O'Fallon, Missouri, constantly enriching their genuine liturgical piety; one of the original associate editors of *Orate Fratres,* who contributed more than 100 articles to this journal; one of the founders and presidents of the National Liturgical Conference; lecturer at St. Louis University. He was called "a perfect host, cheerful, helpful, respectful of others' views" and "a towering and impressive figure of great faith and enthusiasm, known less for his writings than for his pastoral sense and integrity." His liturgical motto was: "Not demonstration but celebration."

The elements of renewal

We must do away with all slovenliness and routine. *"Sancta sanctis,"* God's things must be done in God's way! Back, therefore, to a holier and worthier celebration of the Christ-life-carrying and Christ-life-imparting mysteries, the holy sacrifice, the sacraments and the sacramentals. Back to the Sunday Mass, 52 times a year. It is the ideal way of celebrating the Lord's death, particularly on the Lord's Day. Back to an active participation by every member of the parish in the prayers and chants of the church. Back to a more earnest preparation and a more joyful announcement of the living word of God. Back to the "homily" patterned after the homilies of the Fathers. Back to the Sunday and feast day vespers. "The people don't come" is no argument. Vespers (or compline) is sung for the glory of God and some of God's children will always come. Back to a fitting celebration of the patronal feast. The name day of the parish must not be neglected. Back to Advent, Lent, and ember days cleansed from lottos, bingos and buncos. In short: Back to a *"sentire cum ecclesia"* [thinking with the church] for the purpose of restoring true Catholic parochial life in the cell of Christ's Mystical Body, the parish.

■ *Address at the first National Liturgical Week, Chicago, 1940*

The parish and the house of God

From without, but especially from within, the parish church must proclaim: "This is God's house, this is the 'workshop of Christ' in which he praises with his redeemed [people] his heavenly Father and in which he brings to his members his Father's love and life." It must proclaim: "This is the 'workshop of the parish,' in which its families and members join their divine head in magnifying God, in becoming united more closely with Christ and with each other, and, by active participation in the divine mysteries, to advance in age, wisdom and grace that they will become ever more and more temples of the living God." Pious rubbish must scrupulously be kept from the church as unworthy of the King of Ages, unworthy of his chosen and kingly priesthood. Dealers in church goods are advised to make a 30-day retreat "in the catacombs," examining their consciences about the positive contribution they are making (or not making) toward Catholic art and architecture. The mystic Calvary, the altar, on which the world-redeeming sacrifice is reenacted, must not be made the target of playful "decoratism." Flowers and candles must serve the altar, not vice versa. We must return to the use of worthy garments which are garments indeed, not stiff boards that remind one of some sandwichman on Main Street. The sanctuary is not the place for acolytical baby shows and wallflowers. Servers are the congregation's proxies. And for the important things of life it is hardly proper to select seven- and eight-year-old babies for proxies. We must remove from the altar steps all fire alarm gongs, which can only make cheap noises. *"Domum tuam, Domine, decet sanctitudo!"* [Holiness is fitting to your house, O Lord!] Persons who know little or nothing about ecclesiastical art should humbly acknowledge it and follow the advice of those who know. May we not express the hope that every bishop will establish a diocesan art commission, made up of truly competent priests and laypersons, to which are to be submitted all plans concerning exterior and interior church decoration?

■ *Address at the first National Liturgical Week, Chicago, 1940*

The parish

All of us want to be radical instruments in the hands of the Holy Spirit: radical, in the sense of going to the root of things, to the root, in particular, of true parochial life. Many things are rising and falling today. But there is one thing that must remain, grow and bear fruit, and that one thing is the parish, the concrete expression of the Mystical Body of Christ; the parish in whose midst the divine head glorifies with his redeemed members his heavenly Father and in which he infuses his life into his members "for the perfecting of the saints, for the upbuilding of the body of Christ, until we all meet in the unity of faith, and in knowledge of the Son of God, until we become fully mature with the fullness of Christ himself" (Ephesians 4:12–13).

■ *Address at the first National Liturgical Week, Chicago, 1940*

Easter Sunday

Alleluia, alleluia, alleluia! The doorposts of our hearts are sprinkled with the blood of the true lamb, who by his death has destroyed our death and by rising has given us life eternal. The Egypt of slavery is behind us, we have entered the land of promise flowing with the milk of the Easter eucharist and the honey of paschal rejoicing. The heavy stone of guilt is removed from the tomb of our soul and our life is hid with Christ in God.

■ *ORATE FRATRES, 1943*

ILDEFONS HERWEGEN

1874–1946   Studied at Rome, Maredsous and Bonn; fundamental views formed through an intensive study of the works of Matthias Joseph Scheeben; "great prince, abbot and lawgiver" of Maria Laach from 1913 until his death; as abbot, wished for his community "nothing less than to center their whole spiritual life on the liturgy of the church"; initiator of the liturgical apostolate in Germany; inaugurated the liturgical weeks for laypersons in 1914; established the Institute of Liturgical and Monastic Studies at Maria Laach in 1931; editor of *Ecclesia Orans* series. Of him a fellow monk wrote: "The great prelate, *grandseigneur* in the best but also past sense of this word, is no longer among us. His monastic virtues, humility, magnanimity, generosity, nobility of heart, forbearance, will live on in those to whom he has restored an insight into, and a love for, the riches of the liturgy as the blessed life of the Mystical Body of Christ."

The preacher and the liturgy

It may be laid down as a general principle that sermons on the liturgy and its spirit are only possible when the preacher as priest has made their contents his own through living the liturgy and when he has come to consider his sacerdotal and liturgical activity in the celebration of the Mass and the recitation of the breviary as the innermost soul of his entire sacerdotal and pastoral activity. Liturgical prayer life cannot be for him but one among many means of personal perfection. Rather it must be the unifying principle of his personality as a priest. All the petitions of the community find a place in his life of prayer and sacrifice. Consequently, everything in him organically and solely tends toward awakening and fostering the divine life in the Mystical Body of Christ through life with the church and, as its guide, in letting it flow upon the members of the community united with him by his word, which now no longer is a learned discourse or an academic teaching but *life* drawn from the life of Christ.

Only in this manner will he come to know the relation between the rich treasures of the liturgy on the one hand and the concrete needs of the community on the other, which the sermon through its connection with objective liturgy, seasonable and free of all stiffness, brings to the fore.

■ *ORATE FRATRES, 1932*

The building and the people

The Christian basilica, quite unlike the pagan temple which was a mere shrine for the deity, was truly the *domus ecclesiae,* the house of the Christian community. The visible edifice well represented the spiritual one of the community itself and both bore the same name, *ecclesia.*

■ *ORATE FRATRES, 1932*

Liturgy, a pattern of life

The Christian attitude makes God the center and end of all human activity. Through sacramental processes the energy of God is implanted in human souls, and thus the secret and source of happiness becomes an inward one from which outward effects proceed in charity and in solicitude for the well-being and happiness of fellow men and women, in the fullest measure that the resources of the individual and of the Christian community permit. Such is the characteristic of all social action that is truly Christian.

Now, it is precisely true of the liturgy that it is essentially theocentric, and at the same time, as we have seen, that it embraces human life in every respect, not only in matters of intimate personal piety but in the entire outward life of the individual and of human society. And thus in our desire to better the modern world we must look to the liturgy, the primitive standard of the Christian mind and the pattern of Christian life.

■ *ORATE FRATRES, 1932*

REYNOLD HILLENBRAND

1904–1979   Priest of Chicago; teacher and seminary rector; ardent promoter of the Cardijn method (observe, judge, act) among lay groups (Young Catholic Students, Young Catholic Workers, Catholic Family Movement) whom he served as national chaplain in the 1950s and 1960s; chairman of the 1948 meeting during which the St. Jerome Society changed its name to the Vernacular Society; vice president of National Liturgical Weeks, 1949–1954 and on its Board of Directors for 15 years; associate editor of *Worship*. His vision was a synthesis of liturgy and social action. During a conversation with Monsignor John Egan a few days before Hillenbrand's death, he broke into tears as he remembered that some people felt he had wasted his life on small groups. Egan says of him, "He had the most meaningful life of all; he had trained an entire generation of priests and laity to understand church and world and had helped prepare groups for Vatican II."

First things first

We might not be as far as we are except for the last sobering decade—with its disillusionment; with its struggle, its suffering; with its revelation of hard realities, too easily overlooked; with its mounting feeling of the necessity of reconstructing this poor, sorry world, of the necessity of a profound renewal of the Christian spirit, of the necessity of a deep appreciation and intensification of our Christian heritage, which is the God-life in us; with its sense of futility in the old trumpetings; with its disclosure of the ineffectiveness of the old emphases.

In the liturgical field this means the tithing of anise and cumin that we have done: the tremendous insistence on the obligation to attend Mass, the tremendous insistence on not coming late to Mass, the tremendous insistence on such minutiae as taking the front pews or not coughing during the sermon; but neglecting the weightier things: scarcely enough insistence on the meaning of the Mass as Christ's death; scarcely enough insistence on our participation in it as members of Christ, the Head, the High-Priest; scarcely enough on active participation, so often called for by Pius XI—these things which would have made the Mass a driving, a compelling interest. The last decade, pitilessly revealing as it has been, has helped us all to put first things first.

■ *Address at the first National Liturgical Week, Chicago, 1940*

Adoration and praise

We need to emphasize the adoring and praising elements in the liturgy. You know the average Catholic as well as I do, and you know the drift of your own prayer life. Even in the case of excellent Catholics, praying is likely to be over-concerned with petition (the "getting God to do our will" tendency), or possibly with contrition. Such a tendency is egocentric, self-centered. It puts so much stress on ourselves. For that reason it is narrowing, unexpansive. It cheapens us as creatures. Praise and adoration, on the other hand, turn us to the Godhead. They take us out of ourselves, take us away from the confining limits of poor human nature and take us instead to the limitless reaches of the infinite, of the great, good God. There is a deepening, maturing, expansive, exalting influence in this God-centric worship.

■ *Address at the first National Liturgical Week, Chicago, 1940*

Liturgy gives responsibility

We cannot be content merely to share in the renewal of Christ's death and resurrection but must bring the effects of it to society—into all of life, into all social relationships: to the Negro, therefore, who cannot find employment, whose housing is cruelly overcrowded, who cannot enter a Catholic school; to the sharecropper who, in the phrase of Pius XI, has no hope of ever obtaining a share in the land; to the workers who earn too little to rise from their proletarian condition to the security of owning property; to the dispossessed laboring masses of the empire-colonies and of the Far East, whose groans mount to heaven. As a case in point, the average industrial wage in India is only $60 a year; we need to remember this after the war. We must bring the effects of the altar to them. Christ died for all; all are beneficiaries of his justice and charity. We sacrifice with Christ; all must be the beneficiaries of justice and charity at our hands.

■ *Address at the National Liturgical Week, Chicago, 1943*

Away from individualism

People the world over are sick of individualism, of being sundered from others, of the tragic loss which comes from thinking and acting alone. They are sick of individualistic, subjective piety because it lacks depth and vision. They are sick of the individualism that has undone so many homes, that has marred even our Catholic schools. People are sick of the individualism that has made of political life an unspeakably sordid thing; sick of the stinking individualism in our economic life that has denied to workers their rightful place in industrial life; sick, above all, of the individualism in international life that has left the world a shambles and now thwarts the efforts to build a peace. The world is sick of individualism and must get over it. That is why in 1941, surveying what had happened and what was necessary, Pius XII said: "In view of the greatness of the disaster which has overtaken the human race, there can be only one solution: Back to the altars and learn." Back to the liturgy to learn our oneness, our corporateness. For the liturgy is nothing if it is not corporate. It is the communal worship of people, their common prayer, their common action because it is their common sacrifice, the sacrifice of the whole Mystical Body.

■ *Address at the National Liturgical Week, New Orleans, 1945*

Mass and action

The fact that the Mass is an action should drive us to apostolic action. Otherwise we leave our religion and the greatest thing it has, Mass, in the realm of the "purely spiritual," with no resulting action.

■ *Address at the National Liturgical Week, Worcester, 1955*

Liturgy and beauty

Liturgy is the most complete embodiment of the beauty of the Mystical Body.

■ *Lecture at the University of Notre Dame, 1958*

Liturgy needs the arts

This is why we need participation; the liturgy must be an experience of the whole human person. This gives liturgy an additional affinity to art. It will invoke the visual and audible, the dramatic and the poetic; the beauty of line, proportion and perspective; of color, of light and shadow; of fabric and texture; of wood and stone and other good, honest materials; of speech and song; of gesture and posture. The liturgy must be human as well as divine. It should have participation and it should have art.

■ *CATHOLIC MIND, 1962*

CECILIA HIMEBAUGH

1892–1979   Benedictine; with Martin Carrabine launched
the very successful Chicago Inter-Student Catholic Action
(CISCA) group on a study of liturgy and the Mystical Body as
the foundation of apostolic work; friend of Virgil Michel;
contributor to *Orate Fratres*.

Mass prayers

There are some Mass prayers whose audacity fairly takes one's breath away if one pauses to ponder their real meaning. . . . [For example,] when the *In paradisum* is sung over our mortal remains, and the church summons the angels and martyrs to conduct us into "the holy city of Jerusalem," unabashed we may meet the welcoming company with our hands full of the fruits we have borne "through our Lord, Jesus Christ," whose greatest desire is that we may thus "fill up those things that are wanting" to his own glorious redemptive apostolate.

■ *ORATE FRATRES, 1936*

Popularizers of the liturgy

I should certainly not try to "sell" the truth that liturgy is pure, disinterested adoration. Nor should I attempt to "sell" the sublime mystical doctrine of the church's espousal with Christ until I had first "sold" the earthly image of it in the form of human love and marriage. But by far the most important definition of popularize is to make "beloved by the people," as a "popular leader," for example. That is, we must present the liturgy in such a way as to captivate their hearts and minds. For instance, our task as popularizers is to make spiritual isolationists glad to find themselves in the intimate company of all their Mystical Body fellow members; to make the one who merely endures that half hour on Sunday an enthusiastic co-offerer of the Mass; to bring the lonely individualist with the union-of-Christ-and-me idea of communion into the fellowship of union-with-one-another-in-Christ; to make the Sunday morning Catholic into a willing every-day-of-the-week covictim with Christ. That's a large order, but it can be filled.

■ *ORATE FRATRES, 1943*

JOHANNES HOFINGER

1905–1984   Austrian Jesuit; a disciple and friend of Josef Jungmann; promoter of kerygmatic theology; for many years a missionary in China then seminary teacher in the Philippines; specialist in catechetics; regular contributor to *Lumen Vitae* and other catechetical magazines in various countries; dedicated to the training of lay catechists; learned Spanish at age 65 in order to do this more effectively among the Hispanic peoples of the United States. At his death, age 79, he was working in the diocesan catechetical office of New Orleans. He was a simple and humble man who radiated the joy and warmth of Christ.

"We cannot live without the Mass!"

The early Christians had a most vivid sense of the fact that their part in the Mass was not only to hear and to look but *to do something,* to carry out a holy action that presupposed the consecration and special powers received at baptism. The real Christian faith and the good will of cate-chumens were not enough to enable them truly to take part in the Mass, and therefore the catechumens were dismissed after the "liturgy of the word." In the sacrificial action itself they could have done nothing more than "be spectators," "assist devoutly." But the missionary church of those ages did not want any spectators at the sacrifice however well-disposed and devout; it wanted only those present who were able to take active part.

This was clearly the opinion of those who made the regu-lations governing worship. But what did the simple faithful themselves think of their own part in the Mass? We have the magnificent testimony of the martyrs of Abilene, near Car-thage. In the persecution of Diocletian, 50 Christians were arrested at the end of the eucharistic celebration. The record of their trial before the proconsul of Carthage, Annulius, has come down to us. The decisive question for all those arrested was the same: Had they actually taken part in the service that preceded their arrest, and if so, why? The authorities would have been satisfied if they had denied that they had taken part, or if they had given some excuse for it on grounds of violence or undue influence. The prisoners were even tortured to "make it easier" for them to give such excuses. But under torture, the lector *emeritus* explained his participation in this way: "We cannot live without the Mass." Felix publicly confessed himself to be a Christian; then the proconsul said: "I asked if you took part in the gathering. Answer this question." And Felix answered: "As if a Christian could live without the Mass or the Mass be cele-brated without Christians! Do you not know, Satan, that it is the Christians who make the Mass and the Mass that makes the Christians, in such a way that one cannot exist without the other?" And the other Christians answered, in the same way, that they had acted as Christians and celebrated the Mass. The form of the liturgy corresponded to this attitude. In every part, it gives evidence of the active participation of the community, from the response of the congregation to the priest's first greeting to the liturgical dismissal of the people, a dismissal which itself presupposes active participants, for passive spectators have no need to be sent away.

■ *WORSHIP: THE LIFE OF THE MISSIONS, 1958*

Liturgical formation for mission

Christian worship formed apostles. There was no direct orientation toward the missionary apostolate. In taking part in the solemn thanksgiving of the liturgy, Christians became aware of the riches of their redemption in Christ, and so, urged by motives of gratitude, they became active heralds of Christ. Have we no need of such heralds today?

■ *WORSHIP: THE LIFE OF THE MISSIONS, 1958*

Christian living is manifest at the liturgy

The liturgy rightly understood is an initiation into Christian living. The liturgy is far more than a ceremony working from without. And so we should strive primarily not for greater splendor in our ceremonies, but for better understanding of the mystery, for greater personal participation. The divine life, here drawn from its sacred source, itself obliges us to a new way of life, as was stated clearly by the great missionary of the primitive church: "Let us walk in newness of life" (Romans 6:4). It is easy to show—and we should insist upon this with our Christians—how Christian charity and humility must accompany an attitude that is truly eucharistic and sacramental. Rich in heavenly gifts, we should, after the example of our God, practice open-hearted charity; since we have received everything as a free gift, we should be the more humble. What light the holy mysteries cast upon our Christian vocation!

C hristian worship opens up the sources of Christian life: the sacraments, the word of God, prayer. The liturgical renewal desires, above all, forms of worship which will foster interior participation in the sacrifice and the fruitful reception of the sacraments. It does not aim—except secondarily—to increase the external beauty of worship but to cause the people to participate in it, body and soul. It desires to put the word of God contained in holy scripture once more at the service of souls, not only by the reading of it in private but also by the public liturgical reading which is an essential element in Christian worship. It is concerned with a profound renewal of the prayer of our Christian communities and of all those who are one with the praying church.

■ *WORSHIP: THE LIFE OF THE MISSIONS, 1958*

Contemplation

T here are many more fields that might be mentioned as needing to be correlated with a fully rounded liturgical education. Let us consider only one: the *spirit of community and of peace* necessary for contemplation. Everything that can contribute to awakening and to deepening the students' sense of Christian community, everything that can help them understand the *value of silence,* and above all to observe it interiorly, will also contribute to their liturgical life. For are not the lack of the sense of community and the lack of the spirit of recollection among the great obstacles that prevent us from penetrating into the spirit of Christian worship?

■ *WORSHIP: THE LIFE OF THE MISSIONS, 1958*

Participation from within

The best new liturgical prescriptions will be fruitless if the active participation of the faithful does not *come from within*. The first question is, therefore, how to create the *spiritual conditions* for this participation. To avoid formalism, catechesis must play a great part in this work. Opening the hearts of the faithful to the liturgical ideal is directly connected with the presenting of Christian principles. And in this work, the following points are of special importance: Christianity ought to bring out the primary necessity for self-giving. We need to awaken in the faithful the understanding of our living union with Christ in his church and our wonderful participation in his death and in his life. We should continually remind our people that truly Christlike devotion means the primacy of love and requires a direct orientation to God; that our mysterious union with Christ, the union that gives Christians their value and dignity, has its source in baptism and is intensified and developed by the sacrament; that our offering of ourselves to our God finds its perfection here below, primarily in our interior, and secondarily in our exterior, participation in the sacrifice of Christ and of the church.

■ *WORSHIP: THE LIFE OF THE MISSIONS, 1958*

CLIFFORD HOWELL

1902–1981   English Jesuit; vigorous preacher of Layfolk's
Weeks; translator of Pius Parsch's *Volksliturgie;* lecturer in
England and the United States; author of the very popular
Of Sacraments and Sacrifice and *Preparing for Easter;* associate editor of *Worship* for many years. Godfrey Diekmann
says of him, "He was the hearty, laughing, logical champion
of the embattled cause [liturgy]; he was deeply spiritual."

Body of Christ

This belonging in the body of Christ (or incorporation, as it is called) is the very basis of what we call liturgy. What I want to emphasize here is the fact that it is only because of incorporation that there is any such thing as liturgy. And it is precisely because we *are* all so incorporated that liturgy does concern all of us (and not just the clergy). The liturgical movement and all that it stands for is but a development in action of this basic doctrine of the Mystical Body of Christ.

Understand that, and you have the key to everything in the realm of liturgy. Be ignorant of that, and all that is liturgy will seem to you just a sort of persnickety pottering with various aesthetic fads for which sensible practical people just haven't got the time!

And so, dear reader, I beseech you to spare no time and trouble to get a vivid grasp of this wonderful doctrine. It is the basis, not only of liturgy but even of Christianity. Master it, understand it, make it a part of your mental outlook and you will be astonished how it will transform and ennoble and lift up and vivify and gladden your whole faith. "Let us thank God, through the Son, in the Holy Spirit," wrote St. Leo in a sermon quoted in the Christmas Office, "for God has made us alive with Christ, that we might be in him as new creatures! Be conscious, O Christian, of your dignity! You are now made a sharer in the divine nature, so do not degenerate to merely natural standards. Remember of whose body you are a member."

■ *OF SACRAMENTS AND SACRIFICE, 1952*

Christian joy

It is clear from many early writings that have come down to us, especially from the way in which their preachers talked to them, that these early Christians were filled with the spirit of joy. They exulted in the conviction that Christ their Lord had liberated them from the death of sin and endowed them with his grace; they triumphed in the knowledge of his victory over the devil; they gloried in the consciousness that he was their head, the firstborn of many. They knew that they were themselves belonging to each other in one body with Christ.

To them Christ was the one mediator through whom they had access with confidence to God. They were elated in the assurance that through him and with him and in him they could offer to God . . . all honor and glory. For them the whole of life was a Godward movement made possible for them by the fact that their triumphant and risen Lord had himself gone to God.

For Christ, then, they lived; in Christ they would die, so that through Christ they might rise again to eternal life with God. These are the thoughts which are constantly expressed in the liturgy.

■ *OF SACRAMENTS AND SACRIFICE, 1952*

WILLIAM HUELSMANN

1884–1944   Pastor of Holy Family Parish, St. Louis; first treasurer of the Liturgical Conference. He had a profound appreciation of the grandeur of divine worship and its supreme importance in all of Catholic life. An oft-repeated motto was: "We must make our homes Catholic, not merely the homes of Catholics." His last exhortation to his parish was "to love all." He died on Good Shepherd Sunday; at his funeral it was said of him that his whole aim in life was to bring his flock back to the green pastures and the refreshing waters of the sacred liturgy.

Solidarity

The most terrible specter which nations are facing today is the economic problem. Its essence is the lack of realization of our interdependence in regard to our physical and moral well-being. There is, without the least doubt, no truth so wonderfully adapted to win the minds and hearts of men and women to this realization as the truth of the communion of saints, our living oneness as members in the Mystical Body of Christ, the spearhead truth of the liturgical movement.

■ *ORATE FRATRES, 1937*

To the Father

No one comes to the Father, but by me" (John 14:6), says our Lord and Savior Jesus Christ. And no one comes to Christ, but by the church. And no one is brought to Christ in the church but by the liturgy. And thus no one comes to the Father, but by the liturgy. The center of the liturgy is holy Mass. Hence there is no more essential work for the pastor than to open up the way to Christ through participation in holy Mass.

■ *Address at the first National Liturgical Week, Chicago, 1940*

Our communion with one another

Do you, when you go to communion, think only of being united with Christ, or do you realize that communion means being united with Christ and with all those who are one with Christ? The answer is precisely what St. Paul tells us in our text: "Because the bread is one, we, though many, are one body, all of us who partake of the one bread."

That the early Christians understood that in communion we are united not only with Christ but with each other, is shown by one of the earliest church prayers, which asked that "God will grant that as the grains of corn scattered over the hillside are collected to form one bread, so the faithful dispersed over the world shall be gathered together into one, by virtue of this heavenly food."

■ *In a homily shortly before his death, 1944*

PLACID JORDAN

1894–1977 Priest of the diocese of Bismarck; director of religious broadcasts for NBC before 1951; correspondent for NC News Service for more than 50 years; contributor to *Orate Fratres;* on the executive committee of the National Liturgical Weeks.

Inclusive language

N o doubt you have noticed a translation error that seems to occur frequently when conciliar documents are published in various languages.

The *"filii"* usually is rendered as "sons." The generic term, of course, should be translated by using either "sons and daughters" or when appropriate, "children (of God)." The kerygmatic import is obvious.

Also in the Masses of a virgin martyr and of a woman martyr not virgin, and in propers like the one of St. Agatha of February 5, the collects refer to the "weak sex" [*sexus fragilis*] which strikes me as being particularly inappropriate in the case of martyrs. The very term "weak sex" to modern women sounds almost offensive, and you will grant it isn't realistic either!

Would not "valiant woman" [*mulier fortis*] be more adequate?

I wonder whether you'd be willing to adopt these two suggestions and present them in your capacity as a consultor to the postconciliar commission on the liturgy. Many Catholic women, I am sure, would be grateful for such an initiative. It ought not to be received with a sneer by those who still don't realize the importance of granting to women in the church a position more dignified than the one now accorded.

■ *Letter to Godfrey Diekmann, 1966*

JOSEF A. JUNGMANN

1889–1975   Inspirer of liturgical and catechetical renewal;
leader in the field of kerygmatic theology; among the foremost liturgical scholars of our day though his early work
was in catechetics; author of numerous works including the
important and influential *The Mass of the Roman Rite* and
The Place of Christ in Liturgical Prayer; editor of *Zeit-
schrift fuer katholische Theologie;* taught pastoral theology,
catechetics and liturgy at Innsbruck in Austria until 1963;
prominent in the international liturgical study meetings;
member of the Consilium for the Implementation of the
Constitution on the Sacred Liturgy. His oft-repeated question was: Do we really preach the gospel?

Handing on the faith

B ut there was a living liturgy. The liturgy was both Christian school and Christian instruction; the liturgy enriched the parents interiorly to such an extent that they were enabled to instruct their children; the liturgy made the Christians coalesce into one community. Through the liturgy, that is, through the word of God which it contains and through the strength of its sacraments, pagan society became a Christian society.

■ *ORATE FRATRES, 1949*

Our offering is one with Christ's

C ould the Christian sacrifice not have been a gift of precious wine poured out in holy places, or the gift of incense burning on coals of fire and ascending to God in sweet fragrance? No, Christ willed that his brothers and sisters offer no less a sacrifice than that which he himself had offered to the heavenly Father, and he willed that they offer it together with him. Day after day, he, as it were, summons us to his holy mount, where he wishes no longer to pray alone, as once during the quiet nights of Palestine; and he places in our trembling hands his own sacrifice, that with him we may together offer it to the Father—as the small child places its hands into those of its mother and together with her reverently offers to God *one* prayer.

■ *ORATE FRATRES, 1950*

Liturgy and holiness

Christians are a holy people set apart from the world, sanctified in the blood of Christ. Yet more, they are a people called to holiness, a people that must constantly strive to be made whole, to become saints: They may never grow weary to labor step by step to achieve likeness with that primal exemplar of sanctity that shines forth for them in Christ. And the school of sanctity, in which they must learn to put on Christ, is the sacrifice which they offer in union with him. As St. Augustine says: "In the daily offering the church through him learns to offer itself."

■ *ORATE FRATRES, 1950*

Assembly through baptism and eucharist

In the creed we profess our faith that God has poured forth the Holy Spirit upon humankind and that in this Holy Spirit God has called together people who constitute a holy *assembly* that is ever sanctified anew, and a people of *saints* because they have issued from the water of baptism and through the bread of the eucharist are ever united anew in holy fellowship. This is how the Christians of early times thought of the church, and this is how we too must again learn to think of it.

■ *WORSHIP, 1955*

Liturgy itself forms Christians

When, week by week, and year by year, the person of our Lord and his deeds were presented to the minds of the faithful, they could not but realize what it means to be a Christian. So long as the faithful understood this language and were moved by it, they could not go astray, even if their knowledge of the contents of the faith were otherwise slight or if they were unacquainted with the finer distinctions being made by theologians. And we can understand how, through centuries, a ministry of souls was possible that knew nothing of any systematic catechesis, in which there was little preaching and that usually by the bishop only, and in which instruction by means of the printed word was not yet possible. Nevertheless, Christianity flourished and was vitally alive—because the great truths of Christianity were learned and were a living experience in the liturgy. If the church did not cease thus vividly to present the person and deeds of our Lord to the minds of the faithful, she actually was doing only what the Lord himself had in his last hours commissioned her to do when he said: "Do this in memory of me." For these words certainly contain the command to perform the sacramental mystery; but they also include a command to his church to enact the mystery in such a way that his faithful will never forget him, nor will ever forget what he is for them: their way, their life, their truth. The liturgy leads to conscious Christian faith!

■ *WORSHIP, 1956*

Shaping all our prayer

The liturgy a guide to Christian prayer? Without any force ever being imposed on the freedom of personal prayer, the faithful necessarily became aware simply by listening to the prayers of the church to which they answered their *Amen,* what our relationship to God really is. The view of the Christian cosmos came alive to the mind's eye again and again, and they learned the correct attitude that befits Christian prayer.

A guide to Christian prayer—the most exalted theme concerning which the church had to instruct her faithful has always been and is the sacrifice of the new law. There is something great and wonderful in the fact that, ever since the earliest beginning of the church, wherever there are Catholic Christians they gather in the houses of God Sunday after Sunday in their thousands and millions in order to assist in the holy sacrifice.

Perhaps there have always been many among them who merely wished to fulfill their obligation of being present. And no doubt there has existed at times a kind of pastoral care which did not attempt more or demand more from the faithful than that they persevere with due reverence until the end of the sacred action.

But if we inquire from the liturgy of the church and study it when its forms were still a part of life, we find that the liturgy itself has always aimed much higher. It always sought to assemble the faithful around the altar as *circumstantes* [surrounding]—obviously not in a geometrical but in a spiritual sense.

■ *WORSHIP, 1956*

The importance of history

The liturgy of the Catholic church is an edifice in which we are still living today, and in essentials it is the same building in which Christians were already living 10 or 15 or even 18 and more centuries ago. In the course of all these centuries, the structure has become more and more complicated, with the constant remodelings and additions, and so the plan of the building has been obscured—so much so that we may no longer feel quite at home in it because we no longer understand it.

Hence we must look up the building plans, for these will tell us what the architects of old really wanted, and if we grasp their intentions, we shall learn to appreciate much that the building contains and even to esteem it more highly. And if we should have the opportunity to make changes in the structure or to adapt it to the needs of our own people, we will then do so in such a way that, where possible, nothing of the precious heritage of the past is lost.

Thus to a great extent we can apply to the history of the liturgy what Cardinal Newman said about another department of history:

"The history of the past ends in the present; and the present is our scene of trial; and to behave ourselves towards its various phenomena duly and religiously, we must understand them; and to understand them, we must have recourse to those past events which led to them. Thus the present is a text and the past its interpretation."

In matters liturgical a knowledge of the original text, or the original form used in the primitive church, while of considerable value, is not our only interest. Nowadays we no longer expend such efforts as did scholars 50 years ago to reestablish the original text from the documents that have come down to us. For we now realize that other forms, which developed in the years that followed, also proceeded from the life of the church. In the same way as the original, or at least in a similar way, they are derived from the inspiration and activity of the Holy Spirit. They tell us of the manner in which those later generations prayed and worshiped, and what they added to the primitive forms out of their own resources. And also, they form the links of a chain connecting our present-day worship with the life and worship of the primitive church. All the links in that chain are important, for only when we possess them all do we have a complete explanation of the present-day form of our divine worship. But it remains true that the first links are the more important, for they determined the course that succeeding forms were to take.

■ *THE EARLY LITURGY, 1959*

Liturgical sources

The most important of the liturgical sources made known at the earlier period (before the middle of the 19th century) are the following:

1. Justin, the philosopher and martyr, who wrote his first *Apology* about 155 AD. Chapters 65–67 contain some precious information about divine service.

2. The *Apostolic Constitutions* is a work which is basically fictitious, purporting to present the decrees which Pope Clement I received from the apostles. This is important for us because in it we do possess an oriental form of the liturgy of the fourth century.

3. The *Mystagogic Cathecheses of Jerusalem*. These catechetical instructions (about 400) are called "mystagogic" because they were intended for the newly baptized; they served to acquaint them with the sacraments or "mysteries." These include an explanation of the Mass that is valuable.

4. Ambrose, *De Sacramentis* [On the Sacraments]. This, too, is a series of catechetical instructions for the newly baptized; they were given by St. Ambrose about 390 and written down in shorthand by one of his audience. A lengthy portion deals with holy Mass and a section of the canon is quoted.

Eighty years ago, these were all the known sources of the primitive Christian liturgy, aside from the parenthetical observations found here and there in the writings of the Fathers.

Added since about 1870 are:

1. The *Didache*, or *Teaching of the Twelve Apostles*, from the beginning of the second century. In it are found the well-known eucharistic prayers, but the precise place and meaning of these prayers is not very clear.

2. The *Apostolic Tradition* of Hippolytus of Rome, written about the year 215. This work gives us a very clear

picture of the church's liturgical life; it also contains the oldest text of the canon of the Mass.

3. The *Euchologion of Serapion*. Serapion of Thmuis was a friend of St. Athanasius; he died about 360. The *Euchologion* or *Prayerbook* was discovered in a monastery on Mount Athos. It contains 30 prayers meant for use in public worship; amongst them is a complete text of the *anaphora*, that is, the canon of the Mass.

4. *Pilgrimage of Egeria*. This is a description of a pilgrimage made about the year 400 to the Holy Land; it is the work of a nun, a native of Gaul. It contains a lengthy description of the church services then in use in Jerusalem, namely, the daily service and the canonical hours, and the Sunday service; the services of Holy Week are detailed with special clarity.

5. The *Catecheses* of Theodore, bishop of Mopsuestia in Cilicia, who died in 428. These, too, are catechetical instructions for the newly baptized and contain a thorough and detailed explanation of baptism and the Mass.

6. The *Testament of Our Lord Jesus Christ* is a work of the fifth century. It is related to the *Apostolic Constitutions* and contains some important liturgical texts.

■ *THE EARLY LITURGY, 1959*

Mystagogy

If the homily is to fulfill the function assigned to it in the Mass, it must always have a more or less mystagogical character. Taking as its starting point one or another theme from divine revelation or Christian life or the liturgy, it should ultimately move to the eucharist being celebrated here and now. It will again and again return to one point or another that has special significance in the eucharistic celebration, as the occasion may suggest. Thus St. Augustine preached on the "Lift up your hearts" on several occasions and drew attention to its deeper significance, notably in the detailed development of this point in Sermon 227. An ancient heritage in the tradition of patristic homilies (as ancient as the *Didache,* 9:4) is the theme of the one bread made of many grains as symbolizing the unity of Christians.

■ *THE MASS: AN HISTORICAL, THEOLOGICAL AND PASTORAL SURVEY, 1976*

Proper celebration is the best catechesis

When all is said and done, we may best invoke the basic principle that Mass properly celebrated is itself the best catechesis. This maxim acquires very concrete and immediate relevance when we recall that in their substance the classic forms of the eucharistic prayer (one of which Hippolytus has preserved for us in his formulary) coincide almost perfectly with the classic forms of the creed, such as the Apostles' Creed. The only difference is in the address: The eucharistic prayer is addressed to God as a grateful act of praise [*praedicatio*] or profession of faith [*confessio*]; the creed is a declaration pronounced before the community of the faithful, before the church.

■ *THE MASS: AN HISTORICAL, THEOLOGICAL AND PASTORAL SURVEY, 1976*

JAMES KLEIST

1873–1949   German-born Jesuit scholar who spent most of
his professional life in the United States; professor of classics
and classical languages at St. Louis University; author of
manuals and grammars of Greek and Latin; editor and
translator of many early church writings, especially the
series, *Ancient Christian Writers*.

Liturgical adaptation

The liturgical movement looks both backward and forward. It looks backward because it wants to learn how the earliest centuries of our era—in other words, primitive Christianity—behaved in prayer and worship; it looks forward because it wants to enrich our modern religious life by what it has seen in the past. We are not, of course, to suppose that all that is older is *ipso facto* better, or that what has been done in the past must needs be done at the present time. External religious worship is a variable entity, and, in appraising the customs of the past, due regard must be paid to the needs and the temper of the church at the time. These needs and this temper are in a state of flux. What is essential must be safeguarded; what is accidental may be shorn off. The kingdom of heaven is like a seed that grows and develops, and its growth depends on the soil in which it grows.

■ *ORATE FRATRES, 1948*

Eucharist and martyrdom

This connection between eucharist and martyrdom is made quite clear in Ignatius' letter to the Romans where he describes his impending death in eucharistic terms, wishing to become "God's wheat and to be ground that I may prove Christ's pure bread." Martyrdom was the perfect flowering of the eucharist. Polycarp stood in the midst of the flames "as bread that is baked," and if we remember that the early Christians were experts in the use of symbolical language, we need not hesitate to see in this expression another reference to the eucharist. Finally, Polycarp longs to be a drop in "the cup of the Anointed." Here we have not only a well-known metaphor for suffering, but also a reminder of the words of the institution of the holy eucharist. In answering the question, then, what made Polycarp

and the Christian martyrs so courageous in the face of torture and death, we should bear in mind that they derived
their strength from the blessed sacrament, in other words,
from Mass and holy communion. Let the reader ponder this
simple truth and he or she will see that, as the eucharist was
the food of martyrs, so the eucharist should give us, too, the
necessary strength for the martyrdom of everyday life.

■ *ORATE FRATRES, 1948*

BERNARD LAUKEMPER

1888–1949   Priest of Chicago; "patriarch" of the Liturgical Conference; in the basement of his rectory the meetings were held which gave birth to the Liturgical Conference, to which he offered courageous leadership for 14 years. It is said that the participation of his parishoners in the liturgy was a monument to his zeal and prudence in carrying out the ideals of the liturgical movement.

The parish does the liturgy

I yet think that we have approached the entire subject of divine worship from the wrong angle. My impression is that the sanctuary is too often considered as a stage on which we perform with only the audience in the pews in mind.

I have learned through much failure and disappointment to look at divine worship as God's work carried on by the parish. With this in mind, it matters less how many are present (although this is of course also most important), but it matters more that the work is done, and done well, and that the *parish* does it. God is the end of our worship, the people are the worshipers; but the people cannot worship well if there is no worthy worship. It will take much time to reintroduce the people to the liturgical forms of worship and to get their ears and mind tuned to the language of God.

Of course, if people are educated primarily in the "give-me" type of religion, they will not understand that praise of God is the essential thing. They will leave any service of praise and adoration with an empty feeling because they have not had enough time to keep God busy with their business. Needless to say, the psalms take care of petitions too, but in a big way, with a view to the community rather than to the individual.

■ *Letter to the editor,* ORATE FRATRES, *1938*

Closing the gap between priest and pews

The parish is the mystical Christ in miniature. The liturgy is the mystical Christ at worship. The Mass is the highest expression of this liturgical activity of the mystical Christ. This is one of the reasons why the faithful are "lay-priests": for they have a rightful share in the liturgical actions.

In practice, however, it is otherwise. The Mystical Body appears to be decapitated. The head alone seems to act; the rest of the mystical Christ is inactive, waiting for the head—the priest—to finish. But the body seeks more and more to be reunited with the head, and all our teaching of a lay priesthood remains without fruit so long as the visible union of body and head is not restored in our worship, principally the Mass.

■ *ORATE FRATRES, 1938*

MAURICE LAVANOUX

1894–1974 Artist, architect, editor; influenced by the work of Gueranger and Beauduin in Paris; member of the executive committee of National Liturgical Weeks; one of the founders of the Liturgical Arts Society and editor of its publication, *Liturgical Arts;* from 1931 to 1972 devoted much of his energy to these two channels for promoting good contemporary art as a valid form of religious expression. He believed that liturgy itself suggests the appropriate liturgical environment.

Environment and art

On more than one occasion I have tried to give some reason for the rather sad state of religious art during the past decades in this country, and I offered as a reason the fact that, in the early days of our country's existence, the immense job of carving out a living from the land was not conducive to the creation of beauty insofar as religious art was concerned. People relied to a great measure on European sources—hence one reason for our inferiority complex, which still exists today. We have only to read, for example, the chapter on "Washington Irving in England" in Van Wyck Brooks' recent book *The World of Washington Irving* to realize how utterly dependent we were on Europe in developing our taste for sham Gothic buildings, Chinese pagodas and Roman temples. Later, as a reaction against this state of affairs, we entered into a period known as the pseudo-Gothic revival. Under the influence of the proponents of the period, a great deal of excellent archaeological work was produced, but this worship of the past smothered creative work and covered the land with stillborn structures, designed according to norms no longer valid. It would be easy, but hardly profitable at the moment, to enlarge on this point. But the hope can here be expressed that we are at last done with such a misunderstanding of our legitimate artistic heritage, and that we are at the beginning of an era.

W hen we emphasize the excellence of the liturgy for the formation of the spiritual life—and, by extension, for our appreciation of the artistic manifestations of a spiritual life—it is not intended to detract from the relative importance of extraliturgical exercises, such as meditation, retreats, examination of conscience. Such exercises have their importance to combat the influence of a certain pagan atmosphere which surrounds us in the world and to prevent us from falling into the rut of indifference concerning the accomplishment of the highest and most moving liturgical functions. As always, it is a question of putting *first things first*. If this is so, it surely must follow that those objects which are used in the performance of the liturgy should be of the first order—in design, quality of material and excellence of workmanship.

■ *Address at the National Liturgical Week, New York, 1944*

The authentic tradition in art

A s the church is a living organism and its liturgy accommodates itself to temporal needs and circumstances, does it not follow that the external and visual manifestations of that liturgy, on the plane of art, are also living organisms that grow and develop, rather than a dead, lifeless organism, disguised as antiquarianism? The development in which tradition functions is accomplished in many ways—dogma, doctrine, discipline devotions, liturgy and the arts. The liturgical development depends on all the others, and the arts are influenced by all the ramifications of other traditions. And since the arts at the service of the church are embedded in the various aspects of Christian life *in time*, there is no reason to expect that art be encrusted in any one period of history, of time.

■ *LITURGICAL ARTS, 1954*

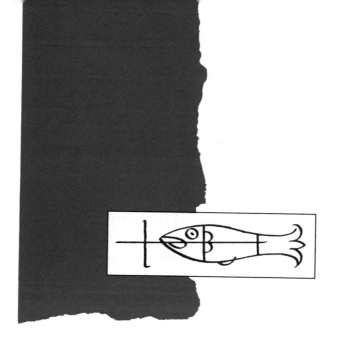

WILLIAM LEONARD

1908–   Professor at Boston College Seminary; founder of
the Summer School of Social Worship on that campus; organizer of the liturgical library at Boston College, which now
numbers more than 18,000 volumes; writer; secretary to the
Liturgical Conference during the 1950s.

Participation in liturgy

Perhaps we should not dwell so much on the labor of the undertaking as on the magnificent prospects that open before us. Think, for instance, of a Sunday congregation that will hear the word of God copiously and in its mother tongue; that will sing its praises, weep for its sins and beg for its necessities consciously and together; that will know, as the Council says, how to offer the spotless victim not only by the hands of the priest, but even with him, and to offer themselves as well.

■ *AMERICA, 1964*

Liturgy and life

It would be a poor liturgical life, however, that would be somehow suspended as we went out of the church, not to be resumed until we entered again. Everything we have seen and heard and done in our worship of God should have had its formative influence on us. We should go out from our community prayer new people, determined once more to publish Christ by our manner of living. If we listen to the word of God humbly and reflectively, will it not instruct us, correct us, shape our basic attitudes, establish for us genuinely Christian values? Can we identify ourselves with the priestly sacrifice of Christ at Mass and then go on living utterly selfish lives? Or how can we sincerely ask for pardon for our sins and then refuse to grant pardon for offenses committed against us? The community worship, in other words, is not offered in a vacuum, but in the living context of our everyday concerns. There should be an overflow from that brimming reservoir of intimacy with God into our individual prayer and into the vigor with which we confront the flesh and the devil.

The liturgy teaches powerfully because it appeals to every sense. It leads us steadily from the known to the unknown, it repeats its lesson over and again in a thousand varied ways. It relates its teaching to our dearest desires and our most secret aspirations; it treats each of us as a distinct and most precious individual; it appeals to the heart as well as the head. "No man ever spoke as this man speaks," the people said after listening to Christ (John 7:46), and in its measure the same could be said of the liturgy. If we want to inculcate an abiding outlook, a culture that will be the well-spring of Christian virtue, we have the instrument at hand.

■ *NEW HORIZONS IN CATHOLIC WORSHIP, 1964*

FREDERICK McMANUS

1923– Priest of Boston; professor of canon law at The Catholic University of America; peritus on the liturgy commission at Vatican II; first American consultant at Vatican II to address his own hierarchy during the time of the Council; director of Secretariat of U.S. Bishops' Commission on the Liturgical Apostolate; editor of *The Jurist* and associate editor of the *Yearbook of Liturgical Studies;* for many years contributor to *Worship;* president of the Liturgical Conference; founding member of the Advisory Committee of the International Commission on English in the Liturgy. In bestowing on him the Berakah Award in 1980, the North American Academy of Liturgy noted: "From pre-Vatican dreams to revised rites, to bound texts, to praying communities, the liturgy was guided with wisdom, conviction and the gentle hands of a friend, a scholar and a man of God."

Standing is a sign of joy

All rise as soon as the consecration is completed with the elevation of the precious blood. This holds true of all sung Masses, whether solemn or high—with the exception of Masses for the dead and most fast day Masses, when all continue kneeling until just before the *Agnus Dei.*

It should be remembered that the normal position of the congregation for the more sacred parts of the Mass—the canon and the communion—is standing; by exception to this, all kneel from *after* the *Sanctus* through the consecration. (See *Roman Missal,* 8:8; 17:5.)

This is not an arbitrary or merely rubrical norm, but the preservation of a most venerable practice of the church. To pray standing is a sign of joy and grace and freedom; from earliest times it has been interpreted as a sign that we are risen with Christ. It is certainly appropriate after the consecration, when we celebrate most solemnly the passion, resurrection and ascension of our Lord and when we join the celebrating priest in the "oblation of the victim placed upon the altar."

■ *WORSHIP, 1959*

Liturgical law

The liturgical movement of this century has been and is the sign of the Holy Spirit's working in the church. But we may wonder how much the liturgical movement would have been needed if the laws and traditions of the Roman rite had been faithfully observed over the centuries.

Popular appreciation of the sacred liturgy would have been vastly different today if, before every administration of the sacraments in the past hundred years, an explanatory instruction had been given, as the Roman Ritual directs; if at every Sunday Mass—there had been the homily or explanation required by the Council of Trent; if at every low Mass the celebrating priest had pronounced loudly and clearly the words which we must now teach the people; if the faithful at a sung Mass had not been denied the right to respond, in violation of the traditions of our rite; if church builders had placed the choir near the altar where it belongs, to lead the people; if baptistries had been erected at the entrances to churches, to signify the meaning of baptismal initiation.

This is only to suggest, by a few examples, how obedience to law has ample motivation in the reasonableness and fruitfulness of the legal precept. And this is nowhere clearer than in the case of sacred worship, where the reverence due to God is at stake and where the sanctity of persons is the profit.

■ *Address at the National Liturgical Week, Notre Dame, 1959*

No ivory tower

When we celebrate the holy liturgy in union with the word of God made flesh, our Lord Jesus Christ, we first hear God's call and then react, respond, reply, with our faith and with our piety. Our liturgy is incomplete if seen only as a human effort of offering, giving, praising; it must include the act of God, making holy, giving life above all human power, sharing the life of Christ. Neither the holy scripture nor the liturgical celebration in which it is enshrined are or may be divorced from our daily life of toil and play. There is no ivory tower for the worshiper who hears God's word; the word of God and the fruits of the liturgical celebration must penetrate our thoughts and deeds, our every social relationship, our place in the society of others.

■ *Address at the National Liturgical Week, Oklahoma City, 1961*

John XXIII *and the coming Council*

W e must thank almighty God for the goodness of the holy father, Pope John. At the very beginning of his pontificate, in what I believe was his first address to clerical students, he laid down the "duty of every priest to assure the liturgical movement a triumphant conquest." His words and actions have fulfilled this duty. And he has made most clear that, since the new code of rubrics is an interim measure which simply could not wait, the basic principles of the general liturgical restoration will be submitted to the fathers of the forthcoming ecumenical council.

In this context and with this encouragement, we can confidently turn to our bishops with the plea, eager and earnest, humble and respectful, that they continue and deepen the liturgical restoration of Pope Pius and Pope John. Assembled in sacred council with the bishop of Rome, our bishops will be true teachers, shepherds and lawgivers. The specifics of liturgical reform have already been laid down in papal documents, in books and journals. We can now seek the solicitude of the fathers of the Council for the flock of Christ and pray that the pattern of liturgical restoration will continue and develop by their solemn decree.

■ *Introduction to the proceedings of the National Liturgical Week, 1961*

The responsibility of the whole church

I f we are doers and teachers, we shall be—like Bernard— counted great in the kingdom of heaven. We may lack the eloquence of the saint in teaching and preaching, in writing and praying. We may not stand up like a tree in the desert, as is said of the saint. But in some sense and in some measure we are all teachers—the priest who preaches; the father and the mother for their children; the clerical, religious or lay teacher of sacred doctrine; each one of us who has a care for our neighbor. We must both keep the commands of the Lord and teach others to keep them.

How else describe this liturgical renewal in which we seek a part than as a teaching, a teaching of the Christian faith manifested and celebrated in the sacred liturgy? This is surely what is meant by speaking of the liturgical movement as a program of education. To spread wider and wider, by word and by sound practice, the clearest understanding of sacrifice, sacrament and prayer—this is the liturgical renewal to which we are dedicated and upon which we concentrate our thoughts during this week. And this spreading of liturgical understanding is an effort of teaching and exposition. It is a task of opening up meanings and depths of Christian worship. It is the office of priest and preacher, mother and father, professional and amateur teacher, religious and lay.

The task is hardly easy. It requires patient study and reflection, such as we shall do during these coming days. It requires constant and perhaps plodding effort, as we try to communicate and to elevate, as we try to teach ourselves and to teach others. We may be only faint, faint shadows of the great doctor of the church, but if we do and if we teach, we may aspire to greatness in the kingdom of heaven.

■ *Homily on the feast of St. Bernard, at the National Liturgical Week, Seattle, 1962*

COLUMBA MARMION

1858–1923   Born in Dublin; abbot of Maredsous; professor of theology at Mont César; described as a "monk of intense inner life, a consummate theologian, a contemplative and apostle of indefatigable zeal." His conferences, centering on the person and work of Christ and published in three volumes, are classics of Christian spirituality. Lambert Beauduin said of him: "Abbot Marmion was before all else a theologian, the complete theologian in the traditional and patristic acceptation of the word; he was not simply a technician in dogma. By virtue of his profound and lively understanding of revealed truth, he was immediately attracted by Christian worship, which involves in its native state, in the lives of the faithful, all those doctrinal emphases which his classical theology taught him needed stressing. That is why his theological science found its authentic and incomparable field of application in the sacerdotal life of the church. He was, in very truth, the theologian of the liturgy."

Psalms and liturgy

S t. Paul tells us "we know not what we should pray for as we ought." God alone knows the way in which we should pray. This is true of the prayer of petition, but it is especially true of the prayer of praise and thanksgiving. God alone knows how God should be praised. The most magnificent conceptions of God formed by our intelligence are human. To praise God worthily, it is necessary that God should compose the expression of these praises. And that is why the church places the psalms upon our lips as the most perfect praise we can, after the holy sacrifice, offer to God. Read the divine pages. You will see how these canticles, inspired by the Holy Ghost, relate, proclaim and exalt all the perfections of God. The canticle of the eternal Word in the holy Trinity is simple, yet infinite; but upon the lips of creatures, incapable of comprehending the infinite, praises are multiplied and repeated.

■ *CHRIST, THE LIFE OF THE SOUL, 1919*

MICHAEL MATHIS

1885–1960   Holy Cross priest; trained in scripture and missiology; expert in Christian Latin; cofounder of the Medical Mission Sisters; founded Holy Cross Mission Seminary; author, founder and editor of Holy Cross mission magazine. In the 1930s, through reading and study of Pius Parsch, he became intensely interested in liturgy. He established the Notre Dame summer sessions in liturgy, started the graduate program in liturgy at Notre Dame and was originator and editor of *Liturgical Studies,* a nine-volume series, of the lectures of the outstanding professors he invited for the summer sessions. Of him it was said, "He gave to the liturgical movement in America a scientific and academic underpinning that won respect for it on all sides and contributed in a major way to American Catholic spirituality."

Liturgy is an art

Liturgy isn't just a science. Of course, it could be treated as such a subject in some universities. Very few institutions have treated the subject not only as a science, but also as an art. That's what liturgy is. It's a living base. In other words, it would be like having a study on chemistry without a few explosions. It would be like studying architecture without ever making a plan. Liturgy is an art as well as a science, and for that reason we have here at Notre Dame made our liturgical programs from the academic standpoint go hand in hand with our liturgical functions.

■ *Lecture given in 1948*

Keeping vigil for Sunday

What strikes me about the Divine Office is that it is the divine word of God heard in the midst of prayer and praise. If we hear God's word in the right atmosphere, something will happen. And that is the whole reason for song in the liturgy. It was in the Old Testament and in the New.

The reason I am interested in the vigil service is that it is the old prayer which the church used to educate its clergy and its people. They had this usually on Saturday night all night and then Mass in the morning. How that marvelous scripture was ordered, no one knows. The history is very cloudy, but it is a marvelous arrangement of the whole plan of salvation, with all its great heroes. The vigil on Saturday nights and on the eve of some major feasts was the prayer life of the people.

■ *Address at the National Liturgical Week, Collegeville, 1957*

THOMAS MERTON

1915–1968   Born in France; educated there, in England and in the United States; entered the Cistercian monastery of Gethsemani, 1941; prolific writer; ecumenist; promoter of contemplative life and social justice in its many aspects.

At peace with time

To understand the attitude of the Christian and of the liturgy toward time we must have a profound understanding of Christian hope and Christian trust. Fundamentally Christians are at peace with time because they are at peace with God. The liturgy also accepts the archetypal, natural image of a "sacred time," a primordial time which mysteriously recurs and is present in the very heart of secular time. Whenever the gospel is sung in the liturgy, it begins with the formula "at that time," and the formula, in effect, destroys the passage of time, annuls all the time that has passed since "then": for in the liturgy the "then" of the salvific actions of Christ is "now" in the redemptive mystery of the church's prayer. It is an affirmation of the fullness of life present.

History itself acquired a new meaning, or rather its hidden meaning was revealed, when the word of God became incarnate and entered into history. Time itself was now an epiphany of the Creator and of the Redeemer, the "Lord of Ages." Yet time also acquired a new solemnity, a new urgency, since the Lord himself now declared that time would have an end.

Time, which is now enclosed between the two advents of Christ—his first coming in humility and obscurity, and his second coming in majesty and power—has been claimed by God for God's own. Time is to be sanctified like everything else, by the presence and the action of Christ.

■ *SEASONS OF CELEBRATION, 1955*

The psalms are poetry

The psalms are poems, and poems have a meaning—
although the poet has no obligation to make his meaning immediately clear to anyone who does not want to make
an effort to discover it. But to say that poems have meaning
is not to say that they must necessarily convey practical
information or an explicit message. In poetry, words are
charged with meaning in a far different way than are the
words in a piece of scientific prose. The words of a poem are
not merely the signs of concepts: they are also rich in affec-
tive and spiritual associations. The poet uses words not
merely to make declarations, statements of fact. That is usually the last thing that concerns him. He seeks above all to
put words together in such a way that they exercise a mysterious and vital reactivity among themselves, and so release
their secret content of associations to produce in the reader
an experience that enriches the depths of his spirit in a manner quite unique. A good poem induces an experience that
could not be produced by any other combination of words.
It is therefore an entity that stands by itself, graced with an
individuality that marks it off from every other work of art.
Like all great works of art, true poems seem to live by a life
entirely their own. What we must seek in a poem is therefore not an accidental reference to something outside itself:
we must seek this inner principle of individuality and of life
which is its soul, or "form." What the poem actually
"means" can only be summed up in the whole content of
poetic experience which it is capable of producing in the
reader. This total poetic experience is what the poet is trying
to communicate to the rest of the world.

It is supremely important for those who read the psalms
and chant them in the public prayer of the church to grasp,
if they can, the poetic content of these great songs. The
poetic gift is not one that has been bestowed on all people

with equal lavishness, and that gift is unfortunately necessary not only for the writers of poems but also, to some extent, for those who read them. This does not mean that the recitation of the Divine Office is an aesthetic recreation whose full possibilities can only be realized by initiates endowed with refined taste and embellished by a certain artistic cultivation. But it does mean that the type of reader whose poetic appetites are fully satisfied by the Burma Shave rhymes along our American highways may find it rather hard to get anything out of the psalms.

■ *BREAD IN THE WILDERNESS*, 1953

Ashes, a sign of resurrection

The cross of ashes, traced upon the forehead of each Christian, is not only a reminder of death but inevitably (though tacitly) a pledge of resurrection. The ashes of a Christian are no longer mere ashes. The body of a Christian is a temple of the Holy Ghost, and though it is fated to see death, it will return again to life in glory. The cross with which the ashes are traced upon us is the sign of Christ's victory over death. The declaration that the body must fall temporarily into dust is a challenge to spiritual combat, that our burial may be "in Christ" and that we may rise with him to "live unto God."

There must be grief in this day of joy. It is a day in which joy and grief go together hand in hand: for that is the meaning of compunction—a sorrow which pierces, which liberates, which gives hope and therefore joy.

■ *SEASONS OF CELEBRATION*, 1955

Experimentation and patience

A great deal is to be done, for it is only a good beginning. All is yet to be fashioned. Not being too much of a pastoral liturgy man, I would not know what to say about all that, except that the singing has got to be really alive and I wonder if the old forms will do? I wonder too if we are yet ready to create new forms that will be "eternal." Better perhaps to envisage a long state of transition and experimentation and hope that plenty of freedom will be granted and properly used!

■ *Letter to Godfrey Diekmann, 1964*

VIRGIL MICHEL

1888–1938   Benedictine monk of St. John's Abbey,
Collegeville; disciple of Lambert Beauduin; brought the
liturgical movement from Europe to the United States; promoted the doctrine of the Mystical Body of Christ; founder
and first editor of *Orate Fratres;* instrumental in establishing
the Liturgical Press; prolific writer; organized the liturgy
summer school at St. John's and the first National Liturgical
Day in 1929. He was an untiring worker, constantly imple-
menting his beliefs and convictions: that liturgy belongs to
the entire church; that the social, liturgical, educational and
biblical apostolates are interrelated; that rural and national
political issues, everything that touches the whole life of the
Mystical Body of Christ, should be of concern to the Christian. To put it in his own words: "Through the liturgy
rightly understood and lived, all our life is centered in Christ
and the Christ-life radiates out into every action of the day."

Liturgy and religious experience

In the liturgy the supernatural truths of faith are expressed in palpable terms, the invisible in visible signs, the divine in human forms, always in imitation, nay in continuation, of Christ himself, the Word made flesh. The liturgy teaches the mind through the senses, the heart through the emotions, the individual by aid of the social, the human through the divine. It answers the whole person, body and soul, heart and mind—and is the one complete and genuine form of the holy grail so earnestly sought today: religious experience.

■ *Quoted by Paul Marx, his biographer*

Liturgy demands participation

The mission of Christ, the mission of the church, the liturgy of the church, all demand contact of the faithful with the living channels of Christ's action here on earth. Without participation of the faithful in the liturgy, these channels have no meaning, no efficacy. But this contact, this participation, is not merely passive, as the very texts of the liturgy also indicate, which incessantly call for active association of the faithful with the action of Christ. While accentuating the hierarchical character of the worship of the church, its intimate connection with the officially delegated ministers of the powers of Christ, the church has not wished to make of it an activity exclusively ecclesiastic. The church has maintained for the faithful an intimate and active participation in the action which the priests perform in the name of all.

■ *THE LITURGY OF THE CHURCH, 1937*

Worship and private devotions

This is indeed an anomaly [dealing with the spiritual life without reference to liturgy] since there can be no truly Catholic life, least of all any such spiritual life, without the liturgy. The latter is "par excellence" the spiritual life of the church and therefore officially also that of the faithful as members of the Mystical Body of Christ.

■ *Quoted by Paul Marx, his biographer*

Learning to do the liturgy is learning Christian life

It is above all the general action of the Mass that should inspire us. There every action of our lives must be centered and thence it must derive its inspiration. If we can learn again to offer our whole selves consciously on the altar of Christ's own sacrifice, our body and our soul, our actions and all the material possessions we have; if we can realize better that this offering is made in union with all our brothers and sisters and is made by each for all and by all for each; and if we can learn to grasp by growing degrees the more sublime truth that this offering of ours is merged with the very sacrifice of Christ himself—then, indeed, shall we be better able to assign to material goods their rightful place in human life and no more; and then too, shall we understand better that all we are and have is most solemnly dedicated to the service of God, to God directly, as well as to the service of God in all our neighbors.

■ *ORATE FRATRES, 1937*

Liturgy, the basis of social regeneration

Pius X tells us that the liturgy is the indispensable source of the true Christian spirit.

Pius XI says that the true Christian spirit is indispensable for social regeneration.

Hence the conclusion: The liturgy is the indispensable basis of Christian social regeneration.

■ *Quoted in* ORATE FRATRES, *1941, three years after his death*

JOSEPHINE MORGAN

1904– Religious of the Sacred Heart of Jesus; musician; studied Gregorian chant at Solesmes with Dom Gajard; director of the Pius X School of Liturgical Music, 1951– 1969; internationally recognized teacher of chant; teacher of music at Manhattanville College for 43 years. During a 1969 celebration in her honor at Manhattanville this tribute was offered: "Her sisters, her faculty colleagues, her students, her friends know that no list can exhaust, can even cover adequately all that she has been to them through the years. Prodigal with her time and energy, her sympathy and her tact, she never turned away from any project, any person whom she could help."

Liturgy and music

Musicians concerned with the liturgy require something in addition to their musical background and the scientific knowledge of church legislation, rubrics and ceremonial. Above all, they must have the spirit of the liturgy, enthusiasm for the true understanding of the liturgy. They must have some insight into the truths of theology and be possessed with the deep spirituality underlying the liturgical services because organist and choir director take such a prominent part in them. A prayerful, reverent sense of the mystery must be in the minds and in the hearts of those who have to watch every step of the liturgical services. Supernatural awareness must be a prerequisite for anyone who conducts a liturgical service. The dryness of routine and repetition and the dullness of spirit which may overtake church musicians must be opposed by prayerful reading and serious study. Without spiritual, intellectual food, liturgical musicians will become dull automatons. Only a great, inspired teacher will be able to inspire others.

■ *Address to musicians at the time of Vatican II, in St. Louis*

JOSEPH P. MORRISON

1894–1957   Priest of Chicago; first president of the Vernacular Society, founded in 1946; a powerhouse in the days when the liturgical movement was considered by many to be a German "invasion"; a practical man; superb in public relations; a genial host.

All are one in Christ

We should as Catholics be able to regard a Negro or Jew or Mexican or a person of any other race, different than ours, without that insensate prejudice which is basically the result of ignorance and error and unbelief. Rather should this fresh evidence of the Creator's power and wisdom, which makes the extremes of exterior human diversity to coalesce in the august harmony of Christ's Body, fill us with feelings of joy, thanksgiving, charity. For in all these souls Christ dwells, sanctifying and strengthening them in precisely the same ways as he does in his contact with us. This mutual sharing of his life and grace should be the groundwork for the structure of spiritual love which is far deeper and stronger than the human charity based upon mere similarity of race or color. For we all are one in Christ, sharing a dignity and an interior beauty of soul that is greater even than that of the angels, for we share the very life of God. So if we allow mere superficial differences of nation or parentage to suffocate that love for all Christ's members that is demanded of us, we injure not only ourselves but also the whole Mystical Body of Christ, and contribute to its decline, to the actual spiritual death of some of its members. For all sin, which is basically uncharity, whether in ourselves or others, connotes the sickness unto death of at least one cell in that living organism. "If anyone says, 'I love God' and hates a neighbor, that one is a liar." So it seems self-evident to conclude that all who bear within them that disease known as race prejudice and make no effort to overcome it are not healthy members of the Mystical Body, but rather ailing ones, who need help themselves and are a drain on the other members. So the answer to the problem, an answer which incidentally seems in accord with our democratic way of thinking, is one based squarely on this basic Catholic doctrine, expressing truly Christian justice and charity. It does not destroy color lines or other racial boundaries or seek to deny or overlook them, but rather does it include and count upon them as further manifestations of the beauty and variety and grandeur which befit that sublime, ineffable reality created by God's love, the Mystical Body of Christ.

■ *Address at the National Liturgical Conference, Chicago, 1943*

Liturgy and daily life

We are urged to reflect seriously and intelligently on the prime importance of the liturgy in our daily life, which should be the Christian life. May God grant that we never lose sight of the nature and *"raison d'être"* of the sacred liturgy. It is the sensible, outward, public process of our public relations with God, of the invisible channels which convey grace to us. One can say that it is the language with which we speak and sing to God, the ensemble of the acts and gestures which we perform so as to put ourselves in relation with God. God grant that we may learn liturgy better, practice it more faithfully, benefit more from its help, and through its use attain everlasting peace and happiness.

■ *Address at the convention of the National Catholic Rural Life Conference, 1950*

THERESE MUELLER

1905– Fled Nazi Germany in 1937 as a young wife and mother; influenced by the liturgical movement in Germany through the abbey of Maria Laach; with her husband, Franz, was befriended by the Catholic Workers in 1938 and through them was introduced to St. John's Abbey, Collegeville; contributor to *Orate Fratres;* author of *Family Life in Christ* and *Our Children's Year of Grace.*

Domestic church

We have become so accustomed to regard a parish as made up of a sum total of separate individual units, men, women, youths and children, that we rather take for granted a sort of vivisection and atomization of the family as the normal and practical way of pastoral work in a large parish. But in truth a parish is not merely a sum total of baptized individuals; it is rather a community of consecrated and grace-dispensing families, empowered by the sacramental graces of holy matrimony. Is it not a beautiful and comforting thought for a pastor to know that he shares his serious responsibilities with so many fathers of families—whom St. Augustine called his "co-bishops"—and so many mothers whose self-sacrificing spirit in all their family cares contributes so greatly in the saving work of Christ our Lord for the world's salvation?

The Christian family, which reproduces in miniature the model of the church at large, is an *"ecclesia domestica,"* a domestic church, a church in the home, a community of love and sacrifice. The wedding day is the day when in the sacrament of matrimony, husband and wife are ordained for their new joint-office in the divine plan of salvation. Thus the wedding day is to be regarded as the beginning of a new phase of religious life, not merely of "happy days" in an ordinary sense, but of exalted days and years.

■ *Address at the National Liturgical Week, St. Paul, 1941*

Family and formation in faith

Pope Pius XI—in his encyclical on education—has called the home "the school of schools," thus emphasizing the dominant position of the home and the parents. In other words, the parents are "the teachers of teachers," the first ones, the original ones to teach, responsible for all other teachers employed by them in the process of education; responsible for all grade schools and high schools, art schools and business schools engaged by them, as it were, to teach certain specialized topics. Parents delegate of their own authority and responsibility to the professional teachers for no other than practical reasons, but are never able to delegate their authority *as such,* their responsibility *as such.*

It is a modern heresy, not yet quite in the open, but nevertheless a heresy, that parents can hand over to professional teachers their own "jobs," their own responsibility, or that professional teachers, youth leaders or whoever is equipped with the required diplomas, can take over from the less equipped (so they say!) parents the formation and education of their children.

Child psychologists are unanimous in stating that the child learns more and faster in the first three years of life than in any later period. And they also agree that the foundation for all education and character formation is laid inevitably in the first five years. This is the very time spent exclusively in the home with parents and brothers and sisters, where there is no other "method" of teaching or learning than living and experiencing. What a loss if in this period of foundation the religious factor is omitted!

Religious education and the formation of a child are a great task and a grave responsibility, but are they not also a holy privilege and the sweetest burden there is?

■ *ORATE FRATRES, 1947*

JANE MARIE MURRAY

1896–1987   Involved in the liturgical movement from 1928
on; collaborator with Virgil Michel and coauthor with him
of the religion text series for elementary and high school:
The Christ Life, Christian Religion and *Christian Life;* associate editor of *Orate Fratres;* teacher at Aquinas College,
Grand Rapids, Michigan; organizer of the Marywood Center for Religious Studies; author of two Holy week booklets
and many articles in catechetical periodicals; lecturer; active
in community renewal after Vatican II; retired from academic life in 1975 and began jail ministry which led to her
being appointed to Michigan's Crime and Criminal Delin-
quency Council in Lansing. At her 75th birthday she wrote
the following: "Each person's growing old is surely distinctly
her or his own thing. It has never happened before. For
'being old' is an age as truly authentic as that of childhood,
adolescence, youth or middle age. It is not merely a negative
condition. There is a 'new' thing that awaits one who is old,
and, as I see it, this new thing lies in the positive loving
acceptance of each experience of declining powers as a special sharing in the saving work of Christ."

Devotion to Mary

To allow Christ to have his way in our lives, in all their details, sometimes calls for heroic courage. We need divine aid to enable us to live up to our high vocation as Christians, children of God. Such aid is given us beyond all measure. This morning our heavenly Father invites all of us to stand about the heavenly table and feast in celebration of the Assumption of the Blessed Virgin. And after the sacred Banquet in which Christ is received, the church asks God that through the prayers of Mary we may be delivered from all the troubles that threaten us. From all the troubles that threaten us! The prayer is for all members of Christ the world over, each of us threatened by troubles peculiar to our individual life. From all of them the church prays that we may be delivered through the intercession of our Mother.

■ *ORATE FRATRES*, *1937*

Lent, an annual retreat

For the whole body of the church to be resplendent on Easter morning it is necessary that each part thereof be beautiful. Since the whole beauty and glory of the Christian life consists in the perfection of charity, it is toward love of God and love of neighbor that the whole labor of Lent is directed. Prayer, fasting and almsgiving are the three chief works of Lent, and of these the first is prayer. Lent is a holy time, a time of annual retreat for the whole church.

■ *ORATE FRATRES*, *1943*

Lenten mortification: charity

The love of God fostered through the daily celebration of the lenten liturgy must be manifested in love of our neighbor. The church has always insisted on charity and forgiveness of injuries as an absolute requirement in preparation for Easter. Concerning the obligation of forgiving injuries, St. Augustine says: "There is no excuse from this good work, since it depends entirely upon the will. One may say that she is unable to fast; another that he would give to the poor but has barely the necessaries of life for himself. No one can say, 'I cannot forgive.' What a grievous thing it is if a Christian would refuse to pardon a brother or sister when we should love even our enemy." Nor is the concern of the church solely for her children. All the nations of the world are her care. Hers is the mission to teach all nations, baptizing them in the name of the Father and of the Son and of the Holy Ghost, and teaching them to observe all things which the Lord has commanded. Like her divine spouse she teaches not only by word but by example to the world: "O God, let the whole world experience and see that that which was fallen is raised up, what was old is made new, and all things are reestablished, through him from whom they received their first being, our Lord Jesus Christ" (Collect after second prophecy, Holy Saturday).

■ *ORATE FRATRES, 1943*

JOHN P. O'CONNELL

1918–1960   Priest of Chicago; assistant to Joseph Morrison in 1943; through Morrison, became involved in the Liturgical Conference as its secretary (even before there was the title); known as "God's gadfly" because of his tireless work for the Conference: editing minutes, writing to speakers, trying to secure new members; editor of missals and prayer books; wrote and lectured on liturgy. His many friends loved him for his simplicity and the genuine warmth of his devotion to them. When told that his death was near, he sat up, looked intently ahead and uttered the last words of the Bible, "Maranatha, come Lord Jesus."

Baptism and worship

We would come closer to an understanding of the Christianized soul after baptism if we would think of all its endowments as powers. The divine life, for example, is the root power to see God face-to-face, a power that will blossom forth in the heavenly vision. The theological virtues are the powers to know, to love and to hope in God. The gifts of the Holy Ghost are powers enabling the soul to be easily moved by the Holy Ghost's inspirations. Likewise, the sacramental character is a power: It enables the Christian to have a part (active or passive) in the liturgy of the church. The character is precisely a liturgical power. For it gives Christians their place in the liturgical worship of God.

■ *Address at the National Liturgical Week, Boston, 1948*

Priesthood and sacrifice

In recent years many crucifixes have represented Christ in priestly robes. This is an attempt to put before the eyes and minds of Catholics a very old conception of Christ as a priest. At the moment of Christ's sacrifice on Calvary a new order, a new life, a new home was established here on earth—the church, the Mystical Body, which is the new kingdom of God. That sacrifice lives on and is daily re-enacted in the church. . . . Christ placed in the church his own sacrifice and enabled all Christians to offer it to the Father. Hence, Christians are a "holy priesthood" (1 Peter 2:5), sharing in the priesthood of Christ. Though all the baptized are in some sense priests, all are not priests in the same way. But whether we speak of the bishop with the fullness of the priesthood, of the ordained priest who is a priest in the strict sense of the word, or of the laity who are priests in a true but wide sense of the word, we must realize what Pius XII reminded us of in *Mediator Dei,* that "to participate in the eucharistic sacrifice is our chief duty and supreme privilege."

■ *Address at the National Liturgical Week, Dubuque, 1951*

PIUS PARSCH

1884–1954   Canon in the monastery of Klosterneuburg near Vienna; led the popular liturgical movement in Austria for 25 years as its foremost pioneer and exponent; founded the *Volksliturgisches Apostolat* press; translated the work of theological and liturgical scholars into language that was convincing *and* attractive, providing spiritual nourishment for daily life; saw scripture and liturgy as complementary, and so provided Bible translation as well as liturgical writings. He might be characterized by the phrase with which he usually ended his letters: "with gentle doggedness."

Praying with the rites

The old priest picked up a copy of the ritual and said to me: "Do you sometimes make a meditation from the ritual?" His unexpected question perplexed me. I did not know what to answer. But I thought for myself "from the ritual?" Why, no one ever told me that one could make a meditation from the ritual. I have never forgotten his question, a question put to me on the day of the heavenly *transitus* of Pius the Great, the Pope who pleaded with the world for a return "to the primary and indispensable source of the true Christian spirit"; to the liturgy, that is, the eucharist, the sacraments, the sacramentals, the Divine Office and the year of the church.

"From the ritual?" Often have I asked myself: "Why wasn't that grand old priest appointed professor of a seminary?" He could have and, I know, he would have told his students for the priesthood something not only about the "technique" but the "mystique" of the missal, breviary and ritual. Writing these lines on All Souls Day, 1947, I wish to lay a fresh wreath of sincere gratitude on the grave of my spiritual guide for the inspiration he gave me, especially by directing me to "meditation from the ritual."

■ *Reminiscence in* ORATE FRATRES, *1947, about two events of August 20, 1914: the death of Pius X and the words of a venerable old priest*

Seasons and play

If we wish to correspond adequately to the liturgy of the church's seasons and feasts we must do two things: understand and utilize. First we have to grasp the whole dramatic character and import of the liturgy, and then we must learn how to apply this to ourselves. Undoubtedly the liturgy is "play," but it is not idle play, not just a game: Underlying this "play" is profound content of grace and truth.

■ *ORATE FRATRES, 1947*

A blessing for the homily

When the priest or deacon prepares to read the gospel of the Mass, bowing deeply or genuflecting he prays that God may consecrate his heart and lips: "Cleanse my heart and my lips, O God, who didst cleanse the lips of the prophet Isaiah with a live coal; deign of thy gracious mercy so to cleanse me that I may worthily proclaim thy holy gospel." Perhaps we have hitherto regarded this blessing of our tongue as a mere empty ceremony, because we have seldom really "proclaimed" the gospel at Mass. We can in the future interpret this rite as a blessing for our liturgical sermon. We will not fail truly to announce the gospel to our people again and again; we will also announce the "glad tidings" in its broader sense through the liturgical sermon and for that we need above all God's blessing and cleansing of our heart.

■ *ORATE FRATRES, 1948*

HANS ANSGAR REINHOLD

1897–1968 Born in Germany; came to the United States in 1936; lifelong friend of Odo Casel and Karl Adam; vigorous in his protest against anti-Semitism and in his expression of concern for every dimension of social justice; his "Timely Tracts" in *Orate Fratres/Worship* were at the forefront of the American liturgical movement from 1938 to 1954; author of six books; a founder of the Vernacular Society. Known to all as HAR, he had the gift of making profound and lasting friendships. One friend said of him: "With many who were able to break through the reserve of his shyness and find in him 'a soul afire,' he generously shared his insights and his love. His vision included the whole of human life, leavened by the reasonable service of liturgical worship."

Vestments

Liturgical revival is not primitivism, nor is it historicism. A full vestment is more of a vestment than the products of the 19th century. Therefore I should prefer ample vestments, if they were very good and modern; they would be the 20th century idea of a sacred vestment. They would be liturgical because they would be fit to be used at *our* liturgy. They do what they are supposed to do: disguise a poor sinner for this holy action in the person of Christ. Christ's grandeur, purity, heavenly splendor and eternity should be made manifest. The people of the 16th and 17th centuries, with their silk, gold, lace and the confusing wealth of baroque architecture and music did succeed in suggesting these traits of Christ. The 19th century wanted an artificial atmosphere of repristination. That was too bad. Our form will be liturgical if we have enough faith to "consecrate" our contemporary beauty and then go right ahead and use what we find.

■ *ORATE FRATRES, 1939*

Fruit of the earth and work of human hands

Bread is something we partake of every day, a thing for every person, a part of our life. It is food, daily food. It makes us grow, be strong and healthy. It comes from farms and has in it the sun, the soil, the rain, the wind and all the good forces of creation. Hard work and human art, a simple and beautiful art, millstone, fire and water helped to prepare it. It is not raw nature, but nature ennobled by our work and intelligence. And then the Holy Ghost has transformed it through divine power. It became the vessel of salvation and spiritual nourishment. That is liturgy: consecration of the true and good things, assumption of created things into the eternal and one sacrifice of creation in its head Jesus Christ.

■ *ORATE FRATRES, 1939*

Becoming liturgical

There is a coherence between life outside and within us, Christ and the world, our mind and the economy of salvation, our person and the church. When we begin to see this, to experience the truth and the fact, we then are consciously living members of the living Christ, the church. Then we realize that the sacraments and the liturgy are functions of Christ, who becomes mysteriously contemporaneous to us, veiled and disguised under appallingly plain symbols —bread, wine, water, oil, words, actions and persons. When all this invades our consciousness, then we begin to understand and we *become* liturgical.

■ *ORATE FRATRES, 1939*

Guests or members?

Transient Christians never become members of a parish and they naturally develop religious individualism or indifferentism. Although many of them could attend Mass wherever they are, they will always be guests and somewhat irresponsible in the community of the parish. The community angle of their spiritual life is being neglected. They are still Catholic, even Roman Catholic, perhaps practicing Catholics. They may give a full share to the upkeep of any parish they come to. But there is an imponderable in our spiritual life which is necessary and which cannot be neglected without damage to our own religious personality. It consists in attachment to the very natural ties which connect us with family life, with a given community, with the soil. We have to rub shoulders with our neighbors, also in religious life, if we want to develop into real religious personalities.

■ *ORATE FRATRES, 1939*

Liturgy and popular devotions

Very often an artificial contrast is construed between liturgy and popular devotion. In these controversies between advocates of liturgical reform and defenders of existing devotions, the latter often make an equation which is by no means valid. To assume that so-called popular devotions are really more popular in their content or style is an assumption that has never been proved. If we spent as much time on liturgy and as much effort on its explanation and translation as we seem able to spend on the introduction of new novenas, liturgy would probably be the "popular" thing.

The assumption that the style of our "devotions" corresponds more intimately to the soul of our faithful is built on the same conception as the other assumption that the products of our religious goods stores on Barclay Street and a certain kind of prayer book literature are more congenial to our people than true art and holy scripture.

Antiliturgists often say: "Liturgy is nothing but an official formula of worship and prayer in our holy church which has to be performed by its clergy, while the people pray out of the fullness of their hearts." They identify public, spontaneous prayer with what we call popular devotions. Is this contrast true?

We all know that a Christian who recites nothing but official liturgical prayer would soon be hollowed out by formalism. Liturgical prayer can only remain genuine prayer if its formulas are an object of constant meditation and assimilation. Private prayers, heart-to-heart communing with our Savior and our Father in heaven, are a prerequisite and have to be concomitant with all liturgical.

There is no conflict between the obligation of private prayer which Christ inculcates in us and the obligation of participation in the liturgical worship of our church. We must have both things if we want to keep liturgy within the realm of our personality and if we want to avoid formalism.

On the other hand we have to have the example and inspiration of liturgy in order to avoid unsound individualism and anarchy in our popular devotions and in our private prayer.

W e have examples of modern devotional language which give us the impression that many of those prayers which are now used by our people have been conceived and composed under the inspiration of a strong personal religious experience of an individual mystic. The language of many of these prayers is very strongly emotional and effusive. This is altogether justified for mystics. But for the average man and woman, this language leads to the falsification of his or her whole prayer life. Verbosity and formalism threaten here more, far more, than in the use of the sober, moderate and healthy formulas of our liturgy. If we compare such strong language with the moderate language of our liturgy, we see right away that something has to be done, not to overstress truth and not to lead the average person into an unnatural and untrue effusiveness. This is certainly true when we have a whole congregation reciting prayers in common. You cannot gear a whole crowd to emotional pitches without creating mass hysteria or empty verbalizing.

Let us sum up what we ought to learn from the liturgy for our own personal prayer and for our extra-liturgical public worship. *First,* its objectivity—we have to learn to leave our narrow personal sphere and ascend to the higher level of the universal church and the universal truth of this church; *second,* dogmatic correctness and a deeper sense of dogmatic proportion; *third,* sobriety and strength; *fourth,* a certain chastity and moderation in language which we are supposed to use in public worship. By this term *chastity,* I mean to say a certain restraint of our language which makes it more fit for the public worship of common people; *fifth,* a greater clarity and precision; *sixth,* an education to truthfulness in our devotional language; *seventh,* a deep sense for the majesty of God. This last is often sadly lacking and superseded by what one could call a sort of "devotional chumminess" with our Lord. Some of our modern devotions lack spirituality in their motive and language which is so admirable in our liturgical prayer.

L et popular devotions, public, popular worship grow. Let it take even more space than it does now, but let it be reflected by the spirit of the church and not by the spirit of commercial efficiency and radio advertising, pseudo-mysticism and slovenliness. Let it be inspired by the one, ordered and only necessary rule of prayer, our holy Roman liturgy.

■ *Address at the first National Liturgical Week, Chicago, 1940*

Laying down our lives

S ince we are members of that Mystical Body, which prolongs the incarnation, the state of the body social is a liturgical concern. We who claim to live by the sacraments must be found in the forefront of those who work for a new society built according to the justice and charity of Christ.

Between shallow activism and naive optimism, this-worldly and natural, on the one hand, and, on the other, an awareness of our duty to lay down our lives for justice's and charity's sake in order to implement what we do in sacred signs, there is a world of difference. The same men and women who beg for more vernacular, who strive for sanctity through a more intense living in the sacramental world of the liturgy and through their ascetic efforts, must be the ones who not only give alms—person to person or in drives —but who help unions, sit on employers' councils and housing committees, in interracial groups and Catholic Action centers, who campaign for the medical services for the strata that cannot afford them, who oppose demagoguery and injustice to the freedoms needed by all people, and who make the cause of enslaved nations a matter of their own heart.

■ *ORATE FRATRES, 1952*

Wild growth is cut away

B ut the Mass is, above all, the Lord's Supper, the memorial of his humanity as well as of his divinity. The mystery should not be sought in rites for their own sake, in an almost folklorish preservation of historical debris, collected by the ebb and flow of the liturgical stream as it coursed through the centuries. The mystery should be sought where it really is: in the symbols chosen by the master — bread and wine, combined with his word. It does not consist in the use of a foreign tongue, however ancient and sonorous that tongue may be, nor in the remnant of a rite which has become as incomprehensible as that with the empty paten, as misleading as that of immixtion or as foreign to the Roman spirit as the two trinitarian prayers.

The proposed changes clarify the essential structure of the Mass, so that each stage develops out of its predecessor. There is no longer the danger of becoming confused by now meaningless rites. The changes will make the Mass more comprehensible (especially in the communion rite) to the parish priest and his congregation. They do not attempt to popularize or colloquialize the Mass and thus lead to anarchy and formlessness. These changes are in the great liturgical tradition, going back to the best sources.

As the Mass becomes more lucid and as the wild growth is cut away, the Mass is most assuredly not stripped of its mystery; rather the mystery is reemphasized and pinpointed, as it were. Our sense of mystery is directed to the mystery par excellence: the proclamation of God's word, the making present of Christ's redemption and that mysterious communal meal which unites the Christian with Christ and welds Christian to Christian in the body of Christ which is the church. This is the place to see the mystery, not in quaint and precious rites that leave the expert mystified and the *mystes* puzzled and despairing. Not all that is, is the best that might be; and the church must have the right to "have pity on the flock."

The reform now under way is superior to preceding ones both in knowledge and motive. As to knowledge: The research of the last decades has put us in a position better than that enjoyed by our predecessors for understanding the essential structure of the mass and the development of the various rites. As to motive: The purpose of the reform of Charlemagne and Alcuin was uniformity, discipline and the personal devotion of the clergy; the purpose of that of Trent was simply to put an end to confusion. But Pius XII, following St. Pius X, wanted to enable the spiritually underfed and thirsting masses to refresh themselves at the "primary and indispensable source of the true Christian spirit," and to make the sacrament a matter of true prayer, to which a feeling of wonderment is only a preliminary step.

■ *BRINGING THE MASS TO THE PEOPLE, 1960*

JOHN ROSS-DUGGAN

1888–1967 Original promoter and longtime secretary of the Vernacular Society, which attracted more than 10,000 members; founder and editor of *Amen* magazine for the Vernacular Society; retired from business to devote energies to this cause; traveled the world promoting the vernacular. *America* wrote, "He must have chuckled at the thought that the prayers at his funeral could be understood by the people, thanks very largely to his full-time dedication to the vernacular cause."

The use of English in worship makes sense

All our religious knowledge comes to us, the laity, by way of the English language—the Bible, the catechism, sermons and instruction, spiritual books, the lives of the saints, spiritual advice. The dogmas and doctrines of the church are conveyed to us in English and explained to us in English. Even if heresy threatened, it would have to be corrected through use of the English language.

All this makes sense and is obvious, but there is a singular exception to this general rule. Unlike all other documents sent out for our use and instruction, the official liturgical rites and prayers still are written and spoken in Latin.

Latin is turned into English for our instruction; why not into English when we pray?

The reason and desire of many laymen and laywomen to worship, at least partially and occasionally in their own language, is inherent in the very notion of language—that the words shall be understood by the person speaking and the person spoken to. In prayer, the latter is almighty God so the condition is only necessary with regard to the person speaking.

We are considering prayer, and prayer is defined in our catechism as the raising up of the mind and heart to God. The early Fathers, in explaining what they mean by prayer, almost invariably describe it as "talking" to or "communing" with God, and St. John Damascene says it is the raising up of the mind to God "with a view to asking proper things from God." Surely all this presupposes that we should know what we are talking about.

But the liturgy is not confined to prayers of petition; it includes a great deal that is addressed to the worshiper by way of instruction or exhortation, passages from holy scripture that may with propriety be described as almighty God speaking to us.

As reason requires that we should know what we are asking when we make our petitions to God, so reverence demands that we should seek to understand when God speaks to us.

This pontificate [Pius XII] and the two preceding it [referring to Pius X and Pius XI] have been remarkable for the stress that these three popes have laid on the active and intelligent participation in the church's liturgy as the primary and indispensable source of the true Christian spirit. It is difficult to see how the popes' wishes are to be carried out by the generality of the faithful unless there is some relaxation of the rigid rule of an all-Latin liturgy.

"Active" and "intelligent" are difficult words to bring into a scheme of things where there is a permanent barrier of an unknown language, and the present holy father has recognized the difficulty, for he has granted the German bishops permission to carry out the rites of the Roman ritual, with the exception of the actual sacramental "form," in the German language.

We have been asking that the liturgy shall be granted the position and status indicated by the original meaning of the word, "the people's work." A work that of necessity is restricted to a small minority of intellectuals cannot properly be called "the people's work."

There are two ways of ensuring that the people shall participate in the liturgy and make it once again their own work. One way, and without doubt the more perfect way, is that all Catholics should learn one universal liturgical language, in our case, Latin. But all know that this cannot be done.

The only other way is so to extend the use of the vernacular in the liturgy that the people can intelligently take their allotted part in the public worship of the church. How far that extension will go is a matter for ecclesiastical authority and the Holy Father has in fact laid down that condition and reserved the decision to the Holy See.

■ *Report to the Vernacular Society, 1950*

LEO RUDLOFF

1902–1982   Born in Duren, Germany; entered the Benedictine abbey in Westphalia; deeply influenced by Lambert
Beauduin during studies at Sant' Anselmo in Rome; in 1938,
sent to the United States to establish a foundation for monks
fleeing the Nazis; appointed prior-administrator of Dormition Abbey, Jerusalem, 1949, and its abbot, 1952; founded
Weston Priory in Vermont, 1952, to receive and train monks
for the Dormition; actively involved in Jewish-Christian dialogue; member of the Vatican Secretariat for Promoting
Christian Unity. At his death his brothers said of him, "He
was a gentle man with a deep trust in the guidance of the
Holy Spirit; he was a man of intellect and dignity."

Liturgy is always a public act

E very eucharist is a public official act, though it be offered without ceremonious pomp and splendor. Strictly speaking a "private Mass" in the sense of a private affair is impossible. The entire church and especially the congregation actually present at Mass together offer the sacrifice with and through the priest.

■ *Writing in Germany, 1934*

Giving praise and thanks

F irst of all it is evident that private prayer needs liturgical prayer as its tutor and guide. Private prayer by its very nature tends to become narrow, individualistic, petty. From the source of the liturgy it receives greatness, a wide horizon, dignity. And that in different ways. First, the liturgy teaches the correct hierarchy of values in prayer. Of the three kinds of prayer—prayer of praise, of thanksgiving and of petition —the praise of God for God's own sake occupies decidedly the first place. I need only mention here the beautiful sentence of the Gloria: "We give you thanks, or we praise you (*eucharistoumen soi,* and the Hebrew equivalent) for your great glory." In private prayer we all too easily forget the duty of praising God for God's own sake, as we are tempted to become self-centered, to put our own little self in the center of our interests, instead of centering them around God and Christ. Then the outstanding prayer in the Mass is the one that gave its name to the holy "eucharist," the great thanksgiving of the preface. It used to include our gratitude for all the benefits of God, those of nature and of supernature. But even in the shorter form that has reached us, it is a splendid witness to the gratitude of persons organized and gathered together in the church.

■ *Address at the National Liturgical Week, New Orleans, 1945*

MARY PERKINS RYAN

1912— Wife and mother; spoke at the early Liturgical Weeks and served on the planning committee; participated in Assisi Conference; author of *Speaking of How to Pray* and other works; editor of the journal, *Professional Approaches to Christian Education.* Her talk at the first Liturgical Week was "Lay Persons Using the Breviary." She brought together the movements for liturgical and catechetical renewal.

True piety

I was once on a train and thought it was a nice day to read the breviary, so I pulled out my little black book and went to work. I didn't mind the conductor collecting the ticket. I know he didn't know what I was doing. And I didn't mind a couple of people who came and sat next to me. But then in the door came a priest and, with one reflex action, I found I was sitting on the breviary and reading a copy of the *Saturday Evening Post*. I wondered for some time why I had done that; now I realize that it was because I was afraid the good father would think I was pious. There is nothing we are more afraid of.

■ *Discussion at the National Liturgical Week, Chicago, 1940*

The vision liturgy gives

A person interested in the liturgy must have no fragmentary interest in the concerns of the church. They are all rooted in the liturgy. It is infinitely sad when someone devoted to the liturgy will minimize an interest in the social doctrine, in rural life, in the racial problems, in international life, in Catholic action. We cannot, of course, have a comprehensive knowledge of all these things, but we must have an interest and a sympathy. When you find a person who is lacking in that interest and sympathy, you have found a person who is imperfectly schooled in the liturgy, who does not understand it in its completeness, who does not have the vision it is able to give.

■ THE SACRAMENTAL WAY, 1948

PAX CHRISTI

SHAWN SHEEHAN

1912 –   Priest of Boston; seminary professor of theology;
began working with the Liturgical Conference in 1944 and
served as president from 1956 to 1959.

Importance of reparation

Despite the fact that we were going through a great national crisis during World War II, we as a Catholic community failed to realize that we had a great task of social reparation to do for the sins of all people. As far as popular piety went, it seemed that the war served only to increase our use of vigil lights and attendance at novena services which, though good enough in themselves, tended to exceed their proper place and value. Instead of the spirit of sacrifice and penance, they seemed to reflect exclusively the desire for individual relief, the concern for personal need. Thus as a national group we did not reach the stage where we could have held a public penitential procession before Mass, as did the church of old in times of crises, in common reparation to God for the sins that brought on the war, that were being committed in the war. Perhaps we are not yet sufficiently aware that, as a community, we are the continuation of Christ on earth, bringing his redemption now to the world, as he did in his day and for all time, so that we can appear as a true Mystic Body offering sacrifice and not merely praying for individual intentions.

But no doubt we are making progress; and perhaps the day is not far distant when, in some great moment of crisis, we may witness the edifying sight of a bishop and his people, marching in a real penitential procession through the city in mourning and fasting, and then offering the holy sacrifice, in common consciousness of the fact that it is reparation that is necessary and supreme, and that our individual comfort in a crisis is not primary.

■ *Discussion at the National Liturgical Week, New Orleans, 1945*

Participation

When the late beloved Michael Mathis was in his last illness, he gave some of us who visited him in the Notre Dame infirmary a little lesson in liturgical participation. When we were giving him our blessing and before we could say the Amen, he would say it, raising himself a little, weak as he was. Still showing a spark of the radiant enthusiasm we had seen so often as he gave us new insights into the liturgy, he would say, "See, you are not going to deprive me of my Amen; that is all I have left."

If we were continually alert to the simple ways in which the liturgical rites themselves provide for participation, we could open up a new view of priestly ministration and of liturgy as worship by the whole community of the faithful.

■ *LITURGY FOR THE PEOPLE, 1963*

Ash Wednesday

Another rite in which the assembly and action of the faithful is the principal sign is the ceremony of the ashes at the beginning of Lent. It is often referred to as "getting the ashes," and at best it seems to be thought of as simply a reminder of death or as some sort of a blessing. What is the full sign in this ceremony? First the faithful assemble to begin the holy season of penance. The choir sings on their behalf a plea for divine mercy. The priest blesses some ashes, asking God that they may be a remedy "for all who humbly implore thee, conscious of their sins, accusing themselves, deploring their crimes in thy sight, earnestly beseeching thy great mercy." Then those who are repentant and seeking God's mercy are to come forward. This is the principal part of the sign. It is a public profession that they are sinners, that they intend to amend their lives and do penance, that they are going to observe the lenten discipline, and that they have confidence in God's mercy dispensed in his church. As they come forward to have the ashes put on their heads by the priest, the choir sings a series of antiphons which express what should be in their minds and hearts. Even when the full ceremony is not carried out, that is, without a choir, it should not be a matter merely of people lining up to get something. It is a sacred event, an encounter with God, an act of worship, and here specifically a public act of penance.

■ *LITURGY FOR THE PEOPLE, 1963*

The act of assembling

As we assemble for Mass, the familiar lesson from St. Paul's letter to the Corinthians is a pertinent warning. Although we do not gather first for a community meal, we have the same obligation to be concerned about each other's needs, and by our failures in this we could become just as unworthy of the eucharistic meal as those to whom St. Paul wrote. At the very least it is required for our sincere coming together that we have been striving to remove from our hearts any hatred, anger or prejudice, and from our actions any dissension, discrimination or other injustices. In a positive way, we should be striving to strengthen the bonds of charity, to make more vital the life of the community in which we live. Even more clearly than our coming together, our praying together imposes this obligation on us. Praying together is a clear sign of oneness of minds and hearts. If we are not trying to attain that oneness it would be a dishonest sign.

■ *LITURGY FOR THE PEOPLE, 1963*

GERARD SLOYAN

1919– Priest of Trenton; professor of religious studies at
The Catholic University of America and Temple University;
received the John Courtney Murray Award of the Catholic
Theological Society, 1981; received the Berakah Award of
the North American Academy of Liturgy in 1986; author;
lecturer on a wide range of topics: morality, Bible studies,
worship, interfaith dialogue, preaching. He was president of
the Liturgical Conference in the early 1960s and served on
the board of directors for many years.

The Bible and liturgy

The Bible is intended to bring us into closer communion with God. It has that power, being something alive and full of energy. It can penetrate deeper than any two-edged sword, reaching the very division between soul and spirit. It can do that only if it is read, however, and read in something of the sequence and development in which it was written. The church's public prayer recognizes no source of suitable converse with God higher than the inspired books.

What must be remembered is that the pieces which compose the mosaic of the spoken liturgy—snippets of psalms, antiphonal echoes, readings short and long—will feed the souls of Christians best only if they know who Romelia was and the weak-kneed Achaz; all that the ark stood for and the temple came to mean; who the long-awaited of the gentiles was, that Jew and gentile might recognize him. The church finds prayer everywhere in the Bible, even where human eyes might look for it least. Early Genesis that is so much disputed, the shocking incidents of the historical books which some call immoral, Maccabees which only Catholics accept as inspired, all find their place in the Divine Office and the Mass liturgy. If it is initially assimilated as it was first dispensed, it then appears richly varied and Christ-laden; if not, then it may forever remain a puzzle and a distraction.

The meat and drink of God's discourse to us is lovingly held out: "All you that thirst, come to the waters: and you that have no money make haste, buy and eat; come, buy wine and milk without money, and without any price. Why do you spend money for that which is not bread, and your labor for that which does not satisfy? Incline your ear and come to me; hear and your soul shall live" (Isaiah 55:1–3).

■ WORSHIP, 1952

Reading the Bible

In Bible reading, Christian dogmas come to life. One does not struggle through abstract propositions; one walks with God and talks with God, sees God at work, now merciful, now just, ever loving. One's whole being is reached, intellect, will, imagination, emotions. David sins and lives to repent deeply; Tobias braves the loss of everything he owns out of reverence for the dead; Jezebel falls to the dogs who lick away her painted smile; Philip grows weary of faith and asks for sight of the one Jesus called Abba; Christ weeps for his dead friend and people say, "See how he loved him."

These things touch us because they have to do with us. God does not speak to human hearts in a series of proof-texts. God employs narrative, suspense, love poetry, prophetic warning, reasoned argument, parable, character portrayal, epigrammatic precept, unparalleled biography.

■ WORSHIP, 1952

Relevance to life?

In somewhat soberer accents than those of the pentecostal blaze, we ask through Jane Frances's merits and prayers that we may trust in the power of God, "since only grace from heaven can overcome all the things that withstand us."

In less than two months time the bishops of holy church will be met in council. It is unthinkable that in an assembly of the size and concern of this Liturgical Week, the events in Rome of next autumn and winter should not loom large in our thoughts. What will be the response of the church, through her teachers, to the challenge of our time? The last 90 years have seen the growth of the human race at an unprecedented rate; it has almost trebled. They have witnessed technological progress the full implications of which not even the foremost men and women of science can guess.

Nation has opposed nation in aggressive and defensive war. Since 1870 [when Vatican I adjourned] the liberty to be human has been accorded to more persons, and taken away from more, than in the whole previous history of the globe. What can possibly be the meaning of the last 90 years? What do the next 90 portend, if there are to be 90?

The press and political leadership of the free world at times ask what the relevance of religion is to all this. They are not especially pleased at times when the answers given concern schools and schooling, sit-ins staged by "agitators," the role of the state in the distribution of wealth, nutrition as the major part of the world population question. It is so much easier to ask in a general way why the world's religions are helpless in the face of the arms race. When religion gives particular answers, it ceases to give popular answers.

Yet the more basic complaint against religion by thoughtful persons who both do and do not profess it is that it gives *no* answers. A recent book called *The Christian Failure* by a former-Communist-turned-priest in Algiers asks, "Why have 2000 years of 'Christian' civilization produced atom bombs and apartheid, strikes in the West and starvation in the East?"

And we, what do we do about the events to follow the 90 years after the Second Council of the Vatican? We gather to sing the praises of a devout, rich woman who reportedly climbed over the body of her 15-year-old son to go off and found cloisters for widows and women in delicate health, and convent schools for those who could pay the fees. Or so it seems.

The question is, of course, is that really what we do today? The anguished question of relevance, of whether Christianity has implications for our times, can be highlighted in terms of the picture we have just drawn. We are tempted to say, with some heat, that in commemorating St. Jane Frances we do nothing of the sort. We gather as a holy people of God, elect but in awe at the mystery of election, limited in outlook in fact, but Catholic by vocation and intention, to offer a sacrifice of praise to the Holy One who is the Father of our Lord Jesus Christ. We do this sacred thing while calling to mind an individual in whom Christ was marvelously imaged three centuries ago: a widow, a woman of prayer, a great servant of her fellows, living a life of charity and continence they would scarcely comprehend.

Relevance to life? It is the very essence of Christianity. Without relevance, Christianity is dead, for its mystery is that God became one of us so that we and our life—this earthly life—could be divinized. Christianity is humanity healed, the slave raised up from the dungheap, the poor given food for body as well as spirit while the rich are sent empty away.

Our holy faith does not look for a terrestrial paradise. But it never forgets that Christianity began with a housing problem, that a decent house in a decent neighborhood is an ordinary necessity for virtuous living. It fights for the right of political self-determination of subject peoples and minority populations. Christianity is at odds with bad prisons, emaciated sufferers from disease, more mouths to feed than there is parental love to care for them. "She reaches out her hands to the poor, and extends her arms to the needy. She opens her tongue in wisdom, on her tongue is kindly counsel." (Proverbs 31:20–26, first scripture reading for the day)

Lest the church seem as smugly efficient as the provident housewife in today's lesson, we turn to the fulfillment of the figure in the reality of the gospel: "The kingdom of heaven is like a treasure hidden in a field. . . . It is like a pearl of great price. . . . It is like a net cast into the sea." It is worth every human effort to come in possession of, yet like everything in this life, where we live by faith and not by sight, ambiguous, inconclusive, a baffling mixture of good and bad, the web of life caught on the rock that is Christ, in a pitiful snarl.

Relevance to life is not *sometimes* the question for the worshiping community. It is *always* the question. If bellies should be filled, and the tide of ignorance turned back, and enemies turned to brothers and sisters, and wars recessed, and children made to laugh, and the great ones of this world become open to each other, the power of the gospel and the eucharistic bread that is its sign may explain it. Nothing else will.

For ours is a faith like that of Madame de Chantal. We know that in Christ all is redeemed, though nothing is as yet finally accomplished. The victory over death is won in bodies that are still subject to death. The risen life is the life we live, though we have yet to be sown in corruption. The conjugal chastity of her marriage, the second chastity of her widowhood, the instruction of the ignorant, the relief of the poor, the liturgy she prayed, were her ways, as they are ours, of hastening the Lord's return. They are the church's ancient way of redeeming the here and now, as we cry out in the certitude of Christian hope, "Lord Jesus, come!"

■ *Homily on the feast of St. Jane Frances Fremiot de Chantal at the National Liturgical Week, Seattle, 1962*

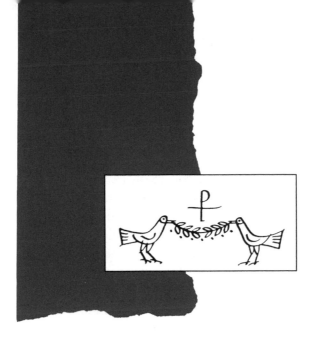

JOSEPH F. STEDMAN

1896–1946   Vice president of the National Liturgical
Conference in 1943; editor of *My Sunday Missal* and *My
Lenten Missal* from which millions of Catholics learned to
pray the Mass (15 million copies in English and translations
were bought and/or donated to the poor of the world). His
great talent for organization and popularization brought him
to work on a Latin-English Roman breviary at the time of
his death.

Participation in the Mass

The Mass, according to the saintly Pius X, is the *"primary and indispensable* source of the true Christian spirit, and the faithful will be filled with this spirit only in proportion as they participate in the sacred mysteries." Notice the words "primary" and "indispensable." All other exercises, private or public, are secondary. The rosary, Benediction, novena services, the way of the cross, all other private and public devotions are very beneficial, but all their efficacy is drawn from the sacrifice of the cross, offered again in every Mass.

In this age of universal reading and inexpensive printing only the *missal should be used at Mass.* All honor to devotions such as the rosary and other devotional prayers, but let them be recited at their proper time, *not during Mass.*

You "will be filled with this spirit only in proportion" as you "actively participate" in the Mass, says Pius X. How do you actively participate? As a layperson you actively participate: first, by *offering the divine victim* to the eternal Father in union with the priest, your official representative; second, by *offering yourself* to the eternal Father in union with the divine victim. To be a co-offerer with the priest, you must have a sacrificial will, so as to make this twofold oblation of Christ and yourself. Your most practical guide, "how to participate," is to recite the same prayers from the missal as the priest.

All during the Mass the missal reminds you that you share in the priesthood of Christ. You too, though *a layperson,* are a "lay priest," to quote many of our liturgical theologians. "You are a royal priesthood," wrote St. Peter to the first Christian converts, both men and women. You have this sublime privilege by the grace of baptism. You have not, indeed, the power of the ordained priest to change bread and wine into the body and blood of Christ, but you can offer the holy sacrifice in union with the priest at the altar. This, then, is the meaning of the plea of the priest at the altar when he turns to the faithful in the pews and says aloud, "Pray, brethren, that my sacrifice and yours. . . ." Too long have people forgotten that they are not merely to assist at Mass but actually to participate in it; *not merely to hear* Mass but to *take a personal part* in it; that the missal is not the private prayer of the priest at the altar, but the collective prayer of all present both in the pews as well as at the altar.

■ *Introduction to* MY SUNDAY MISSAL, *1937*

BASIL STEGMAN

1893–1981   Monk of St. John's Abbey, Collegeville; among Virgil Michel's first collaborators on *Orate Fratres;* assisted Paschal Botz and William Heidt in compilation of *A Short Breviary* in 1941.

The life of the church

When we bear in mind that with God's people in the days of the Old Testament, as even among pagan nations ancient and modern, there is no such separation of religion from life, that their entire life is deeply penetrated and ordained by their belief and sense of responsibility towards the Deity—we wonder how in our Christianity such a distinguishing outlook came about. The answer must be sought in the history of Christian instruction. As long as the faith was taught by living it, and not merely or chiefly by means of the dead letter—introducing the distinction between the mere lesson and its application—then the life of the church was the school wherein the members were truly educated, reared to conform their every conduct to the mission of the church, the sanctification of all for the glory of God.

■ *ORATE FRATRES, 1933*

The psalms

From the days of the apostles, through the years of the catacombs and persecution, during the golden patristic eras, in the flourishing periods of monastic life and religious institutions—throughout the centuries we always find the psalter one of the main sources of inspiration in the life of the church. Hardly a rite or ceremony of her grand liturgy is without some leaven from the psalter. The sacrifice of the Mass is interwoven with the inspired psalmody. The administration of certain sacraments and sacramentals is enhanced by the use of psalms. The psalms were originally the outpouring of private devotion, but because of their universal character they became, already in the ancient temple-worship, the prayer of the whole nation. Thus divested of their individual purpose they became even more in the Christian liturgy the *"vox ecclesiae"* [voice of the church].

■ *ORATE FRATRES, 1936*

GEORGIA STEVENS

1871–1946   Member of the Religious of the Sacred Heart of Jesus; music educator; professional violinist; cofounder of Pius X School of Liturgical Music and its director for 30 years; studied at the Hoch Conservatorium, Frankfurt; author of music textbooks; devised a system for teaching small children to read music, to sing and even to compose. She was loved and revered for the richness of her personality, zest for life, good humor and her ability to produce both a "mirthquake" and "music which flowed silkenly under her directing force." Her obituary concludes: "Hers was a powerful love of God; music was her offering to God, and she would offer God none but the best. Anything less was a desecration of her ideal. It was an inspiration to see her humility before God—an extraordinary quality in a character by nature so headstrong and dominant. She who would flash sparks at the dropping of a *Liber,* would accept a really grave setback with a quiet, 'It's the will of God.'"

Chant with children

You will find, as you come to know Gregorian chant better, that you will love it more and more, until finally you will prefer it to all other kinds of music for the Mass and for the other beautiful services of the church. Gregorian chant seems to express what the words of the liturgy say, so that, when we sing the chant as we should, we are praying and, as we must always remember, praying in the very way in which our holy mother the church wants us to pray. Pius X said that we should "pray in beauty." When we sing the chant well, we "pray in beauty."

■ *From her music text for children, 1944*

Where did chant come from?

To speak intelligently of the chant, we must go back to its birth and early years. It was born with the Christian church in a golden age and spoke the language of that great age. It is characterized by simplicity, which is generally the result of depth—a simplicity that is artless but full of suggestion. It voices the sufferings and the triumphs of human beings in their greatest moments. What are these moments? They may be those illuminated by points of vision, of light; or they may be those that accompany the supreme effort to hold on through utter blackness, hopelessness, in the void, when nothing but the will acts—for the will does act, as it has power to act, in dire need. What has this to do with the chant? Everything. Its birth pangs were in the ecstasy of a great revelation and in martyrdom implemented by pagan cruelty—when the soul was lifted to heaven, the body given to beasts in the arena. It has retained its inheritance, its power to carry a message of hope and of love.

Our own day curiously resembles the early centuries of the Christian era—we too live in a great age of learning and art, and yet the world is torn today as it was then by the onslaughts of barbarians.

Perhaps the differences, however, are greater than the likenesses. In our day we have the radio, and I rejoice at the glorious power that gives so much to the world, to rich and poor; yet it robs us of a precious thing—silence. There always is loss in gain, and here it is a loss in some sense of the creative, communing spirit, which thrives in silence and travails secretly in the necessity of bringing forth something out of the soul's hunger.

■ *CATHOLIC CHOIRMASTER, 1944*

ANSELM STOLZ

1900–1942   Benedictine; German theologian, especially interested in the relationship of theology and piety; professor of dogmatic theology at Sant' Anselmo in Rome. He believed in the cardinal role of liturgy in the full flowering of the divine life in us. One of his students, whose doctoral dissertation Stolz directed, still spoke of him after 50 years as an outstanding and inspiring professor whose "theology of the heart" influenced his whole life.

Mysticism is the natural flowering of the sacramental life

For the mystical life to be truly fashioned on the basis of cult it must be governed by the fundamental ideas of Christian worship, which it thereupon deepens and develops. The mystic will in turn be enabled to perform the liturgy or to take part in it in an especially perfect manner and every conflict between mysticism and liturgy will be avoided. There have been mystics, we know, who have fitted the whole of their interior life into the schema of the sacramental-liturgical life. St. Mechtild of Magdeburg (d. 1285) could therefore conceive of the spiritual life as a holy "octave" of which seven days are spent here on earth and the eighth with Christ in eternal bliss.

■ *ORATE FRATRES, 1943*

SAMUEL STRITCH

1887–1958   Appointed bishop of Chicago in 1939; first
Liturgical Week (1940) held in Chicago under his patronage;
came to see that closer and more formal cooperation with
other religious denominations was needed. He was a gregarious and well-loved figure who humanized the institutional
structures.

Against spiritual individualism

Would it be a mistake to say that there has come about in some Catholics a sorry spiritual individualism somewhat comparable to the tragic social irrational individualism in human society? A failure to understand and appreciate the liturgy seems to have weakened the community conscience of some Catholics who fail in realizing that supernatural life for the Catholic is participation in the inner life of the church and think of it as an isolated supernatural phenomenon of their private lives.

■ *Welcome address at the first National Liturgical Week, Chicago, 1940*

The corporate nature of the church

Religion and its prayerful expressions must not be confined to the privacy of the bedchamber, to secluded nooks and corners in which we shut ourselves off from communion with our neighbors. Our piety must not be that of the modern Puritan, whose idea of "personal goodness" has contributed perhaps more than any other single factor toward the complete secularization of modern society, in its total dissociation from the interests of one's neighbor. Our sanctification is achieved, we should never forget, through a social organism which is the church, in which we as members of the mystic Christ are members one of another. This great supernatural society is precisely God's plan for the salvation of the entire human race; and the piety of this church, the mind of the church is essentially of a social, corporate nature, which we learn to understand and appreciate above all through our participation in her great act of worship, the eucharistic sacrifice, joining with her and with the entire company of the redeemed in offering a perfect act of praise and thanks and reparation and petition to the infinite majesty of God.

■ *Homily at the first National Liturgical Week, Chicago, 1940*

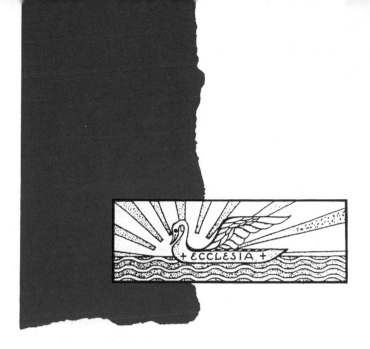

KATHRYN SULLIVAN

1905— Member of the Religious of the Sacred Heart of Jesus; research professor of sacred scripture at Manhattanville College for 46 years; author of many articles, translations and books; on advisory board and regular contributor to *Worship* from the time it included a scripture section until the establishment of *Bible Today,* of which she was co-founder; member of founding editorial board of *Catholic Biblical Quarterly;* self-taught in her field of expertise because women were not admitted to advanced degree programs in scripture and theology; international lecturer on scripture and archaeology; recipient of Edith Stein Award for Judeo-Christian Relations; first woman to hold office in the Catholic Biblical Association. Carroll Stuhlmueller, recalling that he never heard a word of bitterness or frustration, described her "always with a touch of graciousness, humor and gospel humility, and an overwhelming giftedness of gospel zeal for the word of God."

Love of the psalms

Christ prays in the liturgy not only in the Mass but also in the Office. We who repeat the psalms so frequently know that they acquire, for those who know how to enter into them, a surprising depth, a marvelous and inexhaustible actuality. The psalms are the songs of the city of God. They are the voice of the Mystical Body. They are the prayer of the whole Christ. We can agree with Cardinal Newman who wrote that the psalms enable us "to breathe Christ." Cassian assures us, and our own experience corroborates his words, that their recitation is a "swift means to the double goal of religious life: the spread of the kingdom of God and the acquiring of perfect purity of heart." St. Basil told his monks that the psalms contain a complete theology, for their subject matter is God: Creator—Redeemer—Sanctifier. They teach us to praise, thank, love and appeal to the one who made us and loves us.

■ *WORSHIP, 1955*

Mary in liturgy

Grace, beauty, queenly dignity and power of intercession make Esther a worthy figure of our Blessed Mother. And the church does not hesitate to apply to Mary some texts from this book. The seventh responsory of the feast of Our Lady of Lourdes is an adaptation of Mardochai's plea to Esther: "Do thou therefore call upon the Lord and speak to the king for us and deliver us from death" (15:3). The eighth antiphon is also from this book: "Fear not, for this law was not made for you but for all others" (15:13). The communion verse in a Mass of Our Lady Mediatrix reads: "Most wonderful are you, Mary, in your countenance is every grace" (15:17).

Three other liturgical texts are worth noting. Mardochai's prayer to his sovereign Lord who is king of all things is read in the lesson of the third Wednesday in Lent. The gradual gives us the theme of this prayer in the words of Psalm 27: "Lord, save your people, and bless your chosen flock. To you I cry aloud, do not leave my cry unanswered, or I am no better than a dead person going down to the grave" (9:1). The offertory of the 22nd Sunday after Pentecost is Esther's prayer as she went to Xerxes and begged God to frame her plea so that the king would look with favor upon her words.

Two final references must be noted. They are phrases that recur in the *Magnificat*. In Mardochai's dream he is shown that the humble are exalted: "God hath put down the mighty from their thrones and exalted the humble" (cf. 11:11) and Mardochai in exhorting Esther reminds her of her lowliness. Like Mary she is one of God's loved ones, "a poor little one of Israel" (cf. 15:2).

■ *ORATE FRATRES, 1956*

"The Lord be with you"

Eight times during holy Mass the priest repeats a phrase from the Book of Ruth. The greeting given by Boaz to his reapers, "The Lord be with you," introduces the prayer of the four main parts of the Mass: at the reading service, at the offertory, at the canon and at the communion. At a solemn Mass the deacon makes this proclamation before reading the gospel and before the dismissal. It also is said at the foot of the altar and before the last gospel.

This liturgical greeting is found in several places in the Bible. Besides its use in the Book of Ruth, we find it in the Book of Judges. When the angel of God appeared to Gideon, he said: "The Lord is with you, O most valiant one" (6:12). The prophet Azarias drew the special lesson that our happiness is measured by our fidelity to God when God admonished

Asa, king of Judah, with the words: "The Lord is with you when you are with the Lord" (2 Chronicles 15:2). When the archangel appeared to our Lady, he said: "Hail, full of grace, the Lord is with you" (Luke 1:28).

These words in the Mass are always an invitation to pinpoint our attention on what is about to take place. They are a reminder that the Mass is the offering of priest and people.

■ *WORSHIP, 1956*

Availability

Is there one value that we can strive to secure and try to communicate to others and which is at the heart of the promotion of liturgical instruction and active participation in the liturgy? I think there is. I have chosen the value that Gabriel Marcel prizes so highly. It is an attractive simplicity, directness, candor, openness to which Marcel has given the name "availability" *(disponibilité)*. To this word we must attach all the levels of meaning that it has for Marcel. He describes availability as an *intense degree of presence and communion*. Presence, in Marcel's philosophy, is not merely conceptual. It is spiritual reality that follows the awareness of being. It is the realization of I as I and of the other as other. It is the beginning of dialogue. It is the condition for genuine intimacy. It is the possibility of the openness of the I to the thou and their reciprocal exchange. This availability which presence makes possible and which leads to dialogical communion is one of the values of the liturgy.

■ *Address at the National Liturgical Week, St. Louis, 1964*

COLUMBAN THUIS

1885–1974   Abbot of St. Joseph's Abbey, Louisiana; visited Solesmes and was strongly attracted to their liturgy —especially chant—which he brought to his own monastery and to others of the congregation during official visitations; one of the founders of the Benedictine Liturgical Conference in 1940.

The liturgical action of Christ and ourselves

In the liturgy, Christ and we form one unit of action. This liturgical action is not from Christ alone, nor from ourselves alone. It is from both Christ and ourselves as fellow workers in one unit—he the greater and causal—we the smaller and helping. This unity of Christ and ourselves in the one Mystical Body of Christ is endowed with aids of divine origin. Some of these aids work with the direct power of Christ himself as through the sacraments. Some work through the power of the Mystical Body, this Mystical Body being the *operans* or worker. Yet even in these aids, we are fellow workers—but working with such wonderful tools that we rise above ourselves to produce heavenly effects.

■ *Discussion at the National Liturgical Week, St. Paul, 1941*

Christ, the liturgist

This liturgical movement is not an innovation but rather a renovation of the true Christian spirit. It is not a departure from, but a discovery of what has always been ours in the sacraments and sacramentals. It is not a recession from, but an accession to, a procession with Christ, who is called by St. Paul in the Epistle to the Hebrews, our "liturgist" (Hebrews 7:2). The motto of the saintly Pope Pius X, the father of our modern liturgical movement, was to "re-establish all things in Christ." If we may venture a rather barbaric but more truthful translation of this motto, as given in the original Greek of St. Paul to the Ephesians 1:10, it would read, "To rehead all things with and in Christ." This is really the essence of liturgy and the liturgical movement: Christ as head worker in our sacraments and sacramentals, we as members, but real assistants.

■ *Homily given at the National Liturgical Week, Denver, 1946*

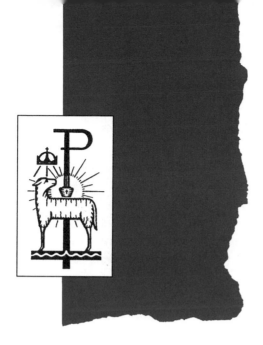

GERALD VANN

1906–1963   English Dominican; possibly the most widely read spiritual writer in the English-speaking world; lecturer; author whose books include: *On Being Human, Divine Pity, Heart of Man;* gave retreats; organized study circles; deeply interested in social and international problems; wrote on the morality of war in 1927; founded a Union for Peace, which joined members of various nations in common prayer for international justice, charity and peace. He once wrote: "Renew your baptism every night, as the dark journey of sleep approaches, begging God to make you love things with God, not against him, as part of your love for God, not as a rival to it."

The double life of symbols

A symbol is a thing with a double life. A beautiful marble statue, a table or a tallboy of well-chosen wood, a goblet of Venetian glass: these have in them the beauty both of material and of form. So a symbol has its own intrinsic nature and beauty—water, wood, wine, fire—but also points beyond itself to a thing or things greater and more beautiful. A *sign* "always has a fixed meaning, because it is a conventional abbreviation for, or a commonly accepted indication of, something known." A *symbol* on the other hand "is an indefinite expression with many meanings, pointing to something not easily defined and therefore not fully known"; it therefore has "a large number of analogous variants, and the more of these variants it has at its disposal, the more complete and clear-cut will be the image it projects of its object." And the church tries to teach us through symbols as well as through doctrine; but we are slow to see and to hear, and much that is of immense value to us, and necessary for us, passes us by. Without a living contact with Christian symbols dogma can very easily become stale and sterile, the meaning rubbed away as from a worn penny; more than that, the "purpose of scientific statement is the elimination of ambiguity, the purpose of symbol the inclusion of it." We decisively need that ambiguity, that ambivalence, if we are to understand the realities of God, of the soul, of the Christian life. So Christ spoke to them in parable, in paradox: You will not truly apprehend the nature of God unless you see him as both just and merciful; you will not understand life unless you see it in terms of both losing and finding; you will not understand purgatory, or the earthly process which the mystics call the dark night, unless you see them as both losing and finding, as both pain and joy.

■ *THE PARADISE TREE, 1959*

ERMIN VITRY

1884–1960 Benedictine monk of Maredsous, Belgium; influenced by Dom Marmion; came to the United States in the 1920s; editor of *Caecilia;* contributor to *Orate Fratres,* including a year-long series of commentaries on the responses and versicles of the breviary; musician, teacher and director of Gregorian chant; music director at the Motherhouse of the Precious Blood Sisters at O'Fallon, Missouri; director of church music programs of the Los Angeles and St. Louis archdioceses; lecturer at Notre Dame summer school of liturgy and at the liturgical music institutes of Boys' Town. The sermon at his funeral included this tribute: "He lived in the awareness of the mysteries of Christ which are also our mysteries. From the abundance of the heart the mouth was ever speaking. In his teaching, in his writings, in ordinary conversation, there was always evident profound reflection on the mystery hidden in God from the beginning."

The sacramentality of sacred music

The sacramentality of sacred music appears the greater if we recall the nature of liturgical prayer. It is by no means the elevation to God of individual Christians separated from their neighbors. It is and can only be the prayer of oneness, which rises from the community bound in Christ's love. Such prayer, because it is "one," and in order to be "one," must needs be dynamic; that is, reaching the highest point of fervor. To this level sacred music, more effectively than anything else, raises liturgical prayer. Thus sacred song becomes the sacramental of fervent and united praise.

■ *ORATE FRATRES, 1951*

Christmas

The Word was made flesh, and he abides in us." Two mysteries are revealed in a single sentence, two mysteries that are correlated as one: Christ's own abiding in the flesh, and then our own abiding in him. This is what we are to see with the evidence of faith.

Take along your versicles, dear reader, and kneel frequently at the crib during the coming season. You need not stay very long, but take the time to look and to look well. This fact, commemorated after two thousand years, made you what you are and decided what you will be forever. Rest awhile by the crib and there contrast the radiant and peaceful lying down of the infant God with the futility of all human endeavor. Then, once again, ask yourself in wonder what it should mean to you. In the calm of this holy night, you will hear in your heart the ringing of these words: "The Word made flesh abides in you." This sentence is the one which has changed the course of the world; it should transform you into a Catholic intimately united to Christ.

■ *Comments on the versicles of the Christmas season, ORATE FRATRES, 1954*

Ascension

As our Lord came down for us, so he returned with us: "He has made captivity captive" [Ascension versicle]. The conquerer of evil now takes possession of the kingdom for his people. With him, we too have ascended, though not fully; for the day of his final coming is still delayed. But, from the throne whereupon he sits, he unceasingly prepares our glorification.

In other words, in the mystery of the ascension Christ is most active and heaven itself becomes the scene of our life. From heaven, all our incorporation into him through the sacraments of the holy church is accomplished by the glorified Christ. And the incessant current of grace which flows from his throne prepares the elect to become the well-polished stones of the eternal city.

Thus, when we speak of our salvation in Christ Jesus, it is of his ascension too that we must think. For ascension is the consummating mystery, not only of the redeemer but of the redeemed. To live in the spirit of this mystery, to prepare as Christ is preparing, is the secret of a full and radiant piety.

■ *ORATE FRATRES, 1954*

JUSTINE WARD

1879–1975   Musician; promoter of Gregorian chant;
author of materials for teaching chant in elementary school;
cofounded Pius X School of Music at Manhattanville College
of the Sacred Heart in 1918 and, assisted by Georgia Stevens,
directed this school until 1931.

The apostolate of church music

W hat struggles to reach this first triumph! For me likewise! I was not a Catholic yet but this papal document
made a profound impression on me and I had already prom-
ised myself that when I was received into the Catholic
church I would work for this good cause.

■ *Letter to Dom Mocquereau about her reaction to the 1903*
motu proprio of Pius X on sacred music

Winged words of eternal life

D uring the past ten years I have had frequent opportunity to observe the formative effect of Gregorian
chant upon young and old, and its infallible power to bring
about a vigorous renewal of the Christian spirit. In a village
of Italy the awful cataclysm of World War II had completely
transformed the people. Everywhere among them there was
discord, strife, quarrels, hatred instead of the unity they had
once known. Religious ceremonies had no meaning for the
people. All contact between the soul of the priest and the
soul of the people was wanting. The great need was to
reconstitute this contact by calling the people to take part in
the Divine Offices, and thus form a group tending towards a
single aim. This miracle has been accomplished by the Gregorian school. The divine prayer of Sunday, intoned with
that lightness, delicacy and soaring quality, ended by uniting
the whole people. All took part in an attitude of devotion. It
was as if Jesus were saying, "Peace be with you." The eucharistic hymn with its solemn and majestic rhythm ended by
enveloping all hearts. The contact was re-established; priest
and people were no longer isolated, and the liturgy had
regained its inexhaustible force in the education of the people. The desire of the church that "the people should take an
active part in the liturgical singing" would be pointless
unless that singing were one of the essential ingredients of a

full Catholic life, unless its vivifying influence were like oxygen to the body, required by each of us, whether rich or poor, talented or not—winged words of eternal life.

■ *ORATE FRATRES, 1927*

Sung prayer

I do not want to talk about sacred music or liturgical music any more. It seems to me that we should rather talk about *sung prayer.*

■ *From her writings, 1929*

Beauty

Day by day, this liturgical splendor unfolded itself before the eyes of the few who assisted, almost as intruders. This beauty concerned them only indirectly. One alone was the object of this consecrated magnificence, this perfection of song and gesture. God, who had created beauty, could be adored only through the full beauty of truth, only through the *Opus Dei,* the "work of God" [liturgy of the hours] to which the monks had dedicated their lives. The sense of that invisible presence animated each note, each phrase, each movement, while clouds of incense rose in spiral designs and, mixing themselves with the sunbeams, entwining their mutual rhythms, executed an aerial dance that flooded the church with rays of perfume and patterns of light.

■ *From her writings, 1950*

Gregorian chant

If chant is not there to make me pray, let the cantors be silent. If chant is not there to appease my inner anxiety, let the cantors leave. If chant is not as valuable as the silence it breaks, let me go back to silence.

■ *Spoken in Paris, 1957*

ALOYSIUS WILMES

1913–1988   Pastor of Sacred Heart parish in Elsberry,
Missouri; secretary of the Liturgical Conference and editor
of many volumes of the proceedings of the Liturgical Weeks.
Wilmes developed his interest in liturgy as an altar server
with Monsignor Martin Hellriegel in O'Fallon, Missouri.

Singing at communion

S inging at communion is especially appropriate, since communion is at the same time communion with the eucharistic body of Christ and communion with his Mystical Body, with our neighbors. We do not communicate alone. It is a family meal, the end of which is not only our personal sanctification, but also unity between the members of the Mystical Body. To sing together is a significant and efficacious means of realizing this unity.

■ *Address at the National Liturgical Week, Portland, 1947*

Reform of the Easter Vigil

M ay we express the hope that what our beloved Holy Father has done with the liturgy of the Easter Vigil gives promise for the future reconstruction of liturgies which suffered equally during the ages. . . . When no one, except the learned, can recognize in the Mass of the Catechumens the worship of praise, doctrine and spiritual preparation for the following eucharist, it is time to stop and examine the cause. When even the scholar can no longer see any resemblance between Christ's last supper and has to borrow far and wide for a relation to Calvary and our present rite of the Mass, then we must all greet with gratitude Pope Pius XII's bold reform of the most beautiful rites of the liturgical cycle of the Roman rite. Especially worthy of note is the delicacy and tact with which this has been done, the respect for tradition, for genuine scholarship of the historian and archeologist, as well as of the laws of liturgical, musical and aesthetic composition. How can we but behold with joy the visible and obvious desire with which the successor of St. Peter inspired his craftsmen when he set the scholars, rubricists, jurists and historians to work—the desire to give the "mother of all vigils" to his people, to make the clergy and people function again in a worship of the people of God.

■ *Address at the National Liturgical Week, Cleveland, 1952*

MARY FABYAN WINDEATT

1910–1981 Member of Third Order of St. Dominic; spent her life in New York writing for the Catholic press; author of many lives of saints for children; contributor to *Worship*.

We receive each other

As baptized Christians, we are really and truly brothers and sisters in Jesus Christ, and when we receive the holy eucharist this union is most perfectly reached, for then we not only receive the King of Kings—in him we receive each other.

Now there is no doubt that many people are not very keen about receiving each other. They have a little complex that revolts against the incorrect grammar their laundress uses, the taste in hats of the woman three pews ahead. They have a regular Great Wall of China of their own—enclosing themselves and acquaintances of similar tastes and capacities.

■ *ORATE FRATRES, 1942*

The secret of communal prayer

Those of us who appreciate an artistic rendering of motets and sacred songs would undoubtedly writhe at having to listen to congregational singing where Mrs. O'Flaherty bungles the Kyrie and deaf old men mispronounce their Latin. But these things are all externals. Always underneath there is the eternal truth—the sense of kinship through Christ that our modern manner of living does so much to thwart. We are all our neighbor's keepers, whether we wish it or not. But until the secret of communal prayer is less of a secret, until something is done to make us nearer, one to another, we shall be strangers, even in our own hearts. For as St. John wrote long ago: "If we do not love our neighbor whom we have seen, how shall we love God, whom we have not seen?" And if we love not God, dwelling in our neighbor, what shall we do, whither shall we go, whom shall we love? And what shall we do about Vespers?

■ *ORATE FRATRES, 1942*

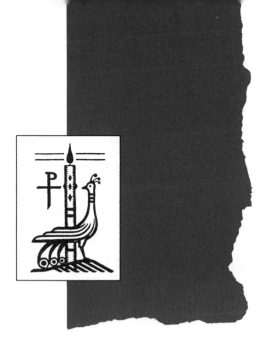

DAMASUS WINZEN

1901–1971   Monk of Maria Laach; fled Nazi Germany to the United States and founded Mount Savior Monastery in Elmira, New York; scholar; served as associate editor of *Orate Fratres;* editor of *Pathways in Holy Scripture;* prime mover in the organization of the Benedictine Liturgical Conference (later known as the National Liturgical Conference).

Chrysostom on the work of the laity

The whole idea of the social participation of the faithful in the Mass is summarized in the following words of St. Chrysostom; "Great, indeed, is the power of the church in her liturgical assemblies. Consider how the force of her prayers freed Peter from his chains and opened the mouth of Paul. These prayers are of no little value to those in higher orders and they help the candidates for the priesthood at their ordination. There is, moreover, no barrier between the priest and those whom he serves; certainly not when one considers the celebration of the sacred mysteries. All are admitted on an equal footing—not as in the Old Law when priests and people ate at a different table; for now the same body and the same precious cup are offered to all. Priest and people unite in intercessory prayers for the infirm of body and of soul, prayers replete with mercy; and in the holy sacrifice itself, what is the meaning of the *'et cum spiritu tuo,'* if not a reciprocal intercession on the part of priest and people? The great act of thanksgiving [known to us as the Canon] is common to both. Remember that the priest does not set out upon this expression of gratitude without first gaining the assurance of the people that the act is fitting and just. Why wonder that the people join with the priest, when one reflects that they unite their voices with those of the angelic choirs in ringing the Sanctus.

"I say these things so that everyone, and in particular the laity, may understand that we are all members of one body, since we differ from each other only as do the members of such an organic whole. Everything should not be left to the priest; rather, all should have the attentive ear that was given to the laity in apostolic times, as for example in the choice of Mathias and of the seven deacons. The church is a spiritual empire, not determined by a hierarchy of titles, but by duties and the cares that superiors are willing to undertake. For all are to dwell in the church as in a home; their affections are to be as those of a single person—and just as there is one baptism and one table and one font and one creation, so too, there is one common Father!"

These are the words of one of the most venerated among the Fathers of the church, the Patriarch of Constantinople and of Antioch and the greatest liturgist of the Eastern Church. May I ask you one question: Is the spirit expressed in these words the perfect realization of the most noble intentions of the people of this country, or is it not?

■ *Address at the first National Liturgical Week, Chicago, 1940*

Liturgical preaching

Our word "preaching" has lost so much of the fullness of its original meaning! The term has absorbed many shades of meaning which we find in the New Testament, but which nowadays we seem largely to have forgotten. One of these shades of meaning which was originally contained in the word "preaching" (as a translation of the Greek *keryssein*) is the public proclamation of the presence of salvation. Preaching is the statement that the world *has* been saved. Preaching is the message of the victory won in battle. Preaching is the proclamation of dominion, the kingdom of the risen Christ. "Christ in you, your hope of glory, him do we preach," says Paul (Colossians 1:27–28).

You can readily see what close inner connection this type of preaching has with the sacramental celebration of Christ's death and resurrection. Therefore liturgical preaching is not only talking about liturgical topics to the congregation, as for example an apologetical proof for the resurrection on Easter Sunday, or a sermon explaining some liturgical rite, the history of ceremonies, etc., but liturgical preaching is that kind of preaching in which the power of the risen Christ is made actual. The sermon preached during the Mass is an integral part of the offering of the sacrifice and a preparation for it. It is not merely a piece of interesting information given to the people. The liturgical sermon is the homily, that is, the friendly, intimate discourse from heart to heart, occasioned by the celebration of the sacrament of unity.

■ *Address at the National Liturgical Week, New York, 1944*

JOHN D. WRIGHT

1909–1979   First bishop of Worcester, 1950–1959; bishop of Pittsburgh, 1959–1969; president of the National Liturgical Weeks, 1954 and 1955.

God's choice of sinners

Christ entrusted the highest offices within his community to sinners. The supreme charge over his flock he gave to Peter who denied him. The first of his evangelists was the publican, Matthew. Last to leave his cross, first recipient of his Easter blessing, was the Magdalen. The foremost of his preachers was Paul, who persecuted the church of God and who acknowledges on his every page his guilt before God and humankind. So has it been ever since in the history of his church. Not the just and innocent, but converted sinners are typically chosen to serve him. All those closest to him except only Mary, his mother, were from among them. She alone was conceived holy in the sight of God.

Again why? Christ chose sinners, even for high places in his apostolate, because there are literally none among all humankind, not even saints, who are not penitents. He did not call into being a special breed of persons to be his priests and prophets and coworkers because in one subtle sense, a sense of which the Holy Saturday liturgy so beautifully reminds us, it was better that those who would be his apostles be themselves sinners. He chose those whom he would send to others from among sinners in order that they might the more persuasively announce his mercy and the better understand the pathos of our sin. His whole plan of redemption required that he restore confidence to souls discouraged by guilt, that he give true peace of mind to lives disordered by sin. Therefore he chose penitent sinners rather than angels to be the preachers of his gospel. For who could better preach the divine mercy than those who personally have tasted it: those who can say with St. Paul that Christ came into this world to save sinners, sinners of whom I am the chief?

■ *Homily at the National Liturgical Week, Boston, 1948*

Sperabamus: A meditation on Emmaus

N o circumstances could be more fitting for meditation
on this gospel than the circumstances of time, place
and condition which find us together. All the world today is
filled with fears; no hearts are more troubled than those of
some Christians. Many who accounted themselves disciples
of Christ or placed their hopes in him now profess that they
are scandalized by things which seem to contradict his
power and to mock his claims. On every side, all over the
world, the aged in their intellectual fatigue, the young in
their emotional bewilderment, question how well-founded
were their beliefs in Christ and their hopes for the coming of
his kingdom. With varying degrees of discouragement,
defeatism and despair, some by their philosophy, some by
their poetry, some by their sociology, some alas, even by
their preaching, echo the bleak existentialism and melan-
choly of the disciples who traveled one evening years ago
from Jerusalem to Emmaus: *Sperabamus!* We used to hope!

We used to hope that the charity of Christ would wipe out
war. We used to hope that the mercy of Christ would cancel
the tormenting memory of sin. We used to hope that the
majesty of Christ would so transcend the boundaries of
racial, national and religious divisions as to unify, fervently
and forever, the scattered tribes. We used to hope that peace
and plenty and the strength of every kind we crave would
surely be ours if only we followed Christ and bore his name.
We used to hope that faith would be untroubled and freedom be untrammeled. We used to hope. . . . But then came
schism, born of politics, and heresy, born of human error.
Came corruption, aggression, rivalry, mutual contempt,
wrath, willfulness and all the sinful progeny of Satan. Came
fascism with its arrogance, communism with its hate, secu-
larism with its cold denials. And Christ seemed driven from

our cities; his gospel seemed absent from our civilization; our hopes seemed vain, our unity was splintered, our faith grew dim, our charity was chilled. . . . *Sperabamus!* We used to hope!

And as we walk with heavy hearts the roads of our escape from supernatural reality, Christ still walks with us. Under the influence of his Spirit, our generation discusses and debates theology in the effort to recover that understanding of Christ that brings with it unity and stability. We turn to "dialogue," as we call it, and at the moment there is none so lost in despair but what he or she puts trust in "dialogue" as the means to the healing of Christendom. But even though Christ be present in the "dialogue" among those who bear his name and who seek to know and love him more perfectly; even though Christ inspires the renewed studies of scriptures, tradition, and the ancient faith which are so characteristic of our times and so encouraging to our hopes, still "dialogue" is not enough, even among the devout.

The accounts of the visions of angels reported by the holy women and the discussion of the prophecies were not sufficient for the disheartened disciples on the road to Emmaus; so too, modern "dialogue" instructs or reminds us about Christ, but in it, too often, we still fail to find him!

But if the contemporary disciples of Christ, if all who bear his name and share the memory of him, unite in acknowledging his supremacy and our need of him, especially as it grows evening and dark around us, then, please God, all Christians shall come to know him fully again in the breaking of the bread.

Jesus reveals his living self in his eucharistic presence; not in mere debate nor "dialogue" alone, but in devotion and eucharistic love is Jesus known. It is here at the altar, in the sacred liturgy, more than in any "dialogue," that the eyes of those who seek him are opened to see him. Yes, in the eucharistic liturgy tonight, in 1960, here in America, Jesus again, and in accordance with his own ordinance, takes bread and blesses and breaks and gives to us—as once he did at Emmaus and as before he did in the cenacle at the last supper—as always he will do until the end of time to unify the body of those nourished by this one bread which makes us one with one another because we are one with him.

As in the days of the first disciples, so today Christ is most vividly and perfectly recognized in the breaking of the bread, in the liturgy, which perpetuates his presence among us in the manner that he ordained. And so, if the first and supreme question is: *What think you of Christ?* the second question, immediately following is: *What think you of this bread that is the eucharist, whose body is it?* The answer to each question contains the answer to the other— and, as at Emmaus, so today, the Christ we recognize in the breaking of the bread is the Christ by whom we are taught in the parables of the gospel, the sermon on the mount, from the pulpit of the cross and through the living church.

It is in the breaking of the bread that we must again come to know Christ. It is in the eating of the bread that we are truly united to him. It is in living by the power of this bread that we grow in the life more abundant and the love undying that the liturgy was given us by Christ to accomplish.

■ *Homily at the National Liturgical Week, Pittsburgh, 1960*

NOTES

All excerpts from *Orate Frates* and *Worship* published by The Liturgical Press, Collegeville, Minnesota, are used with permission. Because of the variety of the authors, the length of time since publication and the brevity of many quotes, it was not feasible to seek out the authors or their heirs to request permission to reprint the quotes. We will be happy in future editions to include any proper and specific acknowledgments.

All excerpts from *National Liturgical Weeks* published by The Liturgical Conference, Washington, D.C., are used with permission. The year given in the citations is the year the Week took place; the proceedings were published in the following year, generally in the city where the executive secretary lived.

KARL ADAM

Excerpts from *The Spirit of Catholicism*, Karl Adam, published by The Macmillan Company, New York, 1935. Copyright © Sheed and Ward, Ltd., London. Used with permission.

CHRIST IN THE LITURGY: *The Spirit of Catholicism*, 19.

PRESENCE OF CHRIST: *The Spirit of Catholicism*, 20.

SACRAMENTS AND HUMAN LIFE: *The Spirit of Catholicism*, 221.

THROUGH CHRIST OUR LORD: "Dogma and Liturgy," *Orate Fratres* 11 (1937): 530–31.

LITURGICAL PRAYER: "Dogma and Liturgy," *Orate Fratres* 12 (1937): 10–11, 14.

DONALD ATTWATER

BANISHING JARGON: "Ecclesiastical Jargon," *Orate Fratres* 1 (1927): 121.

A BLARING OF SAXOPHONES: "Liturgical Revival in England," *National Liturgical Week*, 1949, 153–54.

TO HUNT, TO SHOOT, TO ENTERTAIN: "Lay People in the Church," *Worship* 30 (1956): 305.

LAMBERT BEAUDUIN

Excerpts from *Beauduin: A Prophet Vindicated*, Sonya A. Quitslund, published by Newman Press, New York, 1973.

Excerpts from *Liturgy the Life of the Church*, Lambert Beauduin, published by The Liturgical Press, Collegeville, 1926. Used with permission.

THE BEAUTY OF LITURGICAL PRAYER: *Beauduin: A Prophet Vindicated*, 24.

THE POWER OF LITURGY: *Liturgy the Life of the Church*, iv.

LITURGY IS FOR ALL: *Beauduin: A Prophet Vindicated*, 16.

NO ARISTOCRACY IN THE LITURGY: *Liturgy the Life of the Church*, 43–44.

THE THEOLOGY OF THE PEOPLE: *Liturgy the Life of the Church*, 105.

WHAT THE LITURGY IS MEANT TO DO: *Liturgy the Life of the Church*, 111.

THE RISEN CHRIST: *Beauduin: A Prophet Vindicated*, 194.

TRIBUTE TO ABBOT GUERANGER: "Abbot Marmion," *Orate Fratres* 12 (1948): 313–14.

RESERVATION OF THE BLESSED SACRAMENT: Godfrey Diekmann, "Altar and Tabernacle," *Worship* 40 (1966): 504.

AMEN: *Beauduin: A Prophet Vindicated*, 238.

FLORENCE BERGER

DOMESTIC CHURCH: "In the Home," *Orate Fratres* 25 (1951): 76, 78.

FILLING OUR HOMES WITH PRAYER: "Making for Christ," *Worship* 26 (1952): 525–26.

ADE BETHUNE

WORKING SAINTS: Judith Stoughton, *Proud Donkey of Schaerbeek* (St. Cloud, Minnesota: North Star Press of St. Cloud, 1988), 108. Used with permission.

FIRST, A REVERENCE FOR FOOD: "On Eating," *Orate Fratres* 15 (1941): 159–62.

IMAGES OF THE FATHER: "God the Father in Christian Art," *Worship* 32 (1958): 160, 162–63, 164.

THE CLASSICAL POSTURE OF PRAYER: Judith Stoughton, *Proud Donkey of Schaerbeek* (St. Cloud, Minnesota: North Star Press of St. Cloud, 1988), 116. Used with permission.

BERNARD BOTTE

Excerpts from *From Silence to Participation*, Bernard Botte. Copyright © 1988, The Pastoral Press, Washington D.C. Used with permission.

READING THE GOSPEL TO THE SICK: *From Silence to Participation*, 61.

THE LANGUAGE OF THE LITURGY: *From Silence to Participation*, 77–78.

THE CONDITIONS FOR LITURIGICAL REFORM: *From Silence to Participation*, 65.

LITURGICAL RENEWAL—A LONG VIEW: *From Silence to Participation*, 168.

CONFIRMATION AND HOLINESS: *From Silence to Participation*, 155–57, 159–60.

THE MOST SERIOUS PROBLEM OF THE REFORM: *From Silence to Participation*, 169–70.

PASCAL BOTZ

THE DYNAMIC APPEAL OF THE LITURGY: "Sic Currite," *Orate Fratres* 10 (1936): 146.

PURPLE PATCHES: "Sic Currite," *Orate Fratres* 10 (1936): 146–47, 149–50.

BREATHING THE AIR OF DIVINE TRUTH: "Creed and Cult," *Orate Fratres* 10 (1936): 493, 495–96.

THE GOSPEL: "The Sword of the Gospel," *Orate Fratres* 17 (1943): 98.

KARL ADAM'S GIFT TO THE WORLD: "Karl Adam: Theologian of Christ," *Worship* 32 (1958): 207.

LOUIS BOUYER

NO EASY COMPROMISE: From *Liturgical Piety*, Louis Bouyer. Copyright © 1955, University of Notre Dame Press. Used with permission.

WORD AND SACRAMENT: *The Word, Church, and Sacraments: In Protestantism and Catholicism*, (London: Geoffrey Chapman, 1961), 74. Used with permission.

THE EUCHARIST MAKES THE CHURCH: *The Church of God* (Chicago: Franciscan Herald Press, 1982), 277. Used with permission.

TO HAVE A COMMON LIFE: *The Church of God* (Chicago: Franciscan Herald Press, 1982), 280. Used with permission.

WILLIAM BUSCH

LITURGY AND MODERN INDIVIDUALISM: "The Liturgical Movement" (Letter to the Editor), *Commonweal*, November 4, 1925. Copyright © 1925, *Commonweal*. Used with permission.

LITURGY AND LIFE: Letter written by William Busch to urge article to be reprinted in *Orate Fratres*. From the archives at St. John's Abbey, Collegeville.

THE LITURGICAL MOVEMENT: *National Liturgical Week*, 1940, 224.

THE INNER MEANING OF THE LITURGY: "About the Encyclical *Mediator Dei*," *Orate Fratres* 22 (1948): 156.

PAUL BUSSARD

THE LORD BE WITH YOU: *The Meaning of the Mass* (Wilmette, Illinois: P. J. Kenedy and Sons, 1942), 59.

INCENSING: *The Meaning of the Mass* (Wilmette, Illinois: P. J. Kenedy and Sons, 1942), 59.

DANIEL CANTWELL

WHAT IS SUNDAY: "What Has Happened to Sunday?" *National Liturgical Week*, 1949, 29.

SUNDAY AND SOCIAL CONCERN: "What Has Happened to Sunday?" *National Liturgical Week*, 1949, 32–33.

JOHN CARROLL

VERNACULAR: *Catholics in America: 1776–1976*, ed. Robert Trisco, "American Liturgical Pioneers," Frederick R.

McManus. Copyright © 1976, National Conference of Catholic Bishops, 155. Used with permission.

THOMAS CARROLL

SOME PROGRESS: "Pius XII and Future," *National Liturgical Week*, 1953, 175.

THE LITURGICAL APOSTOLATE: "Pius XII and Future," *National Liturgical Week*, 1953, 176–77.

ODO CASEL

Excerpts from *The Mystery of Christian Worship*, Odo Casel, published by Newman Press, Westminister, Maryland, 1962.

THE MYSTERY OF WORSHIP: *The Mystery of Christian Worship*, 39–40.

LITURGY AND SYMBOL: *The Mystery of Christian Worship*, 46–47.

THE CHURCH YEAR: *The Mystery of Christian Worship*, 67–68.

DOROTHY CODDINGTON

TEACHING CHILDREN: "Let Those Who Can, Do," *Orate Fratres* 19 (1945): 437.

CATECHESIS FOR CHILDREN: "Which Psalms for Children?" *Orate Fratres* 23 (1949): 555.

PATRICK CUMMINS

IMPORTANCE OF THE HOMILY: "Liturgy and Literature," *Orate Fratres* 4 (1930): 499.

ENTRANCE SONG AND PROCESSION: "Sacred Texts and Sacred Songs," *Caecilia* 71 (Omaha: Roncka Brothers, 1944), 90–91. Reprinted by permission of Msgr. Francis Schmitt, Aloys, West Point, Nebraska.

DOROTHY DAY

THE POWER OF THE NAME: Margaret Quigley, *The Dorothy Day Book,* 79–80. Copyright © 1982, Templegate Publishers, Springfield, Illinois. Used with permission.

COMPLINE AT CATHOLIC WORKER: Excerpt from *Loaves and Fishes* by Dorothy Day. Copyright © 1963, Dorothy Day. Reprinted by permission of Harper and Row Publishers, Inc., New York.

ORDINARY TIME: Margaret Quigley, *The Dorothy Day Book,* 109. Copyright © 1982, Templegate Publishers, Springfield, Illinois. Used with permission.

WHY GO TO MASS: Robert Coles, *Dorothy Day: A Radical Devotion* (Reading, Massachusetts: Addison-Wesley, 1987), 76–77. Used with permission.

CATHERINE DE HUECK DOHERTY

THE EUCHARIST AND LOVE FOR THE POOR: "I Saw Christ Today," *Orate Fratres* 12 (1938): 309–10.

ALCUIN DEUTSCH

LITURGY, THE PRIMARY SOURCE: *National Liturgical Week,* 1940, 165–66.

TOTAL PARTICIPATION: *National Liturgical Week,* 1940, 166.

WHAT WE MEAN BY "LITURGY": "The Liturgical Movement," *Orate Fratres* 1 (1927): 391–92.

GODFREY DIEKMANN

THE INTERPRETATION OF LITURGICAL LAW: *National Liturgical Week,* 1941, 189.

FED BY GOD'S WORD: "Living with the Church in Prayer and Reading," from *1955 Proceedings of Sisters' Institutes of Spirituality,* ed. Leonard Collins. Copyright © 1955, University of Notre Dame Press. Used with permission.

ACTIVE PARTICIPATION: "The Chief and Indispensable Source," *Participation of the Laity in the Liturgy of the Mass* (Washington, D.C.: The National Council of Catholic Men, 1955). A radio address, The Catholic Hour, April 3, 1955.

THE PASCHAL MYSTERY: "The Church Year in Action," *North American Liturgical Week,* 1958, 15.

THE DYNAMISM OF THE EUCHARIST: "The Theology of Worship," *Theology Digest,* Summer 1962, 140–41. Used with permission.

THE DEPTH OF CHANGE: From a November 8, 1963, interview with Godfrey Diekmann when he was serving as a peritus for Vatican II. The interviewer is not named; he could be Vincent A. Yzermans. Can be found on tapes in the library of St. John's Abbey, Collegeville, Minnesota. This quote is at the end of Tape 3 and the beginning of Tape 4.

THE PROBLEM OF LARGE PARISHES: "The Eucharist Makes the People of God," *North American Liturgical Week,* 1965, 111.

BAPTISM'S RIGHTS AND DUTIES: "The Constitution on the Sacred Liturgy," from *Vatican II: An Interfaith Appraisal,* ed. John H. Miller. Copyright © 1966, University of Notre Dame Press. Used with permission.

DANGERS IN REFORM: "The Theology of Liturgy According to Vatican II," *Crisis in Church Music* (Washington, D.C.: The Liturgical Conference, 1967), 27. Used with permission.

WORSHIPING WORTHILY: "Reform of the Catholic Liturgy: Are We Too Late?" *Worship* 41 (1967): 150–51.

GREGORY DIX

ANAMNESIS: Excerpt from *The Shape of the Liturgy,* Dom Gregory Dix. Copyright © 1945, Dom Gregory Dix. Reprinted by permission of Harper and Row Publishers, Inc., New York.

LITURGY AS THE PATTERN: Excerpt from *The Shape of the Liturgy,* Dom Gregory Dix. Copyright © 1945, Dom Gregory Dix. Reprinted by permission of Harper and Row Publishers, Inc., New York.

MICHAEL DUCEY

THE LITURGY AND TIME: "Holy Mass, the Great Educator," *National Liturgical Week,* 1947, 74–75.

FINALLY, SILENCE AND FEW WORDS AND HOPE: "Holy Mass, the Great Educator," *National Liturgical Week,* 1947, 79.

BENEDICT EHMANN

COMMUNAL LIFE OF THE CHURCH: *National Liturgical Week,* 1940, 9.

THE MEANING OF PIETY: "The Liturgy and Personal Piety," *National Liturgical Week,* 1944, 32.

THE ALPHABET OF GOD'S MEANING: "The Liturgy and Personal Piety," *National Liturgical Week,* 1944, 35–36.

GERALD ELLARD

SOCIAL SANCTIFICATION: "Liturgy as Social Sanctification," *National Liturgical Week* (Washington, D.C.: The Liturgical Conference, 1946), 47–51. (cf. *Liturgical Arts,* 6, 1 [1936], 6.) Used with permission.

PERFECT PROFESSION OF LOVE: "The Great Sacrifice," *National Liturgical Week,* 1947, 35–36.

ROMANO GUARDINI

Excerpts from *Sacred Signs,* Romano Guardini, published by Pio Decimo Press, St. Louis, 1956. Used with permission.

THE SIGN OF THE CROSS: *Sacred Signs,* 13–14.

KNEELING: *Sacred Signs,* 20.

BREAD AND WINE: *Sacred Signs,* 67–68.

STANDING: *Sacred Signs,* 21–23.

DOES LITURGY HAVE A PURPOSE?: *The Spirit of the Liturgy* (Mission Hills, California: Benziger Publishing Company, 1931), 85–86, 105–6. Used with permission.

PAUL HALLINAN

Excerpts from *Days of Hope and Promise,* ed. Vincent A. Yzermans. Copyright © 1973, The Liturgical Press, Collegeville. Used with permission.

LITURGICAL RENEWAL AND COURTESY: "Church's Liturgy: Growth and Development," *North American Liturgical Week,* 1964, 97.

THE LITURGY IS FOR THE PEOPLE: *Days of Hope and Promise,* 63.

THE FREEDOM TO CREATE: *Days of Hope and Promise,* 195.

ON LITURGICAL COLLABORATION: *Days of Hope and Promise,* 198.

THE AMERICAN CONTEXT OF LITURGICAL RENEWAL: *Days of Hope and Promise,* 224–25.

MARTIN B. HELLRIEGEL

THE ELEMENTS OF RENEWAL: *National Liturgical Week,* 1940, 32–33.

THE PARISH AND THE HOUSE OF GOD: *National Liturgical Week,* 1940, 37–38.

THE PARISH: *National Liturgical Week,* 1940, 38.

ALLELUIA: *Orate Fratres* 19 (1945): 97–98.

ILDEFONS HERWEGEN

THE PREACHER AND THE LITURGY: "Liturgy and Preaching," *Orate Fratres* 7 (1932): 25–26.

THE BUILDING AND THE PEOPLE: "The Liturgy a Pattern of Life," *Orate Fratres* 6 (1932): 511.

LITURGY, A PATTERN OF LIFE: "The Liturgy a Pattern of Life," *Orate Fratres* 6 (1932): 513.

REYNOLD HILLENBRAND

FIRST THINGS FIRST: *National Liturgical Week,* 1940, 5.

ADORATION AND PRAISE: *National Liturgical Week,* 1940, 21.

LITURGY GIVES RESPONSIBILITY: "The Spirit of Sacrifice in Christian Society," *National Liturgical Week,* 1943, 106.

AWAY FROM INDIVIDUALISM: *National Liturgical Week,* 1945, 12–13.

MASS AND ACTION: "The Mass as the Source and Center of the Lay Apostolate," *North American Liturgical Week,* 1955, 179.

LITURGY AND BEAUTY: From the Notre Dame University Archives, Msgr. Reynold Hillenbrand Collection 21/13.

LITURGY NEEDS THE ARTS: "Art and the Liturgy," *Catholic Mind* 60 (New York: America, 1962), 43.

CECILIA HIMEBAUGH

MASS PRAYERS: "Do We Know What We Ask?" *Orate Fratres* 10 (1936): 257, 259.

POPULARIZERS OF THE LITURGY: "Popularizing the Liturgy," *Orate Fratres* 17 (1943): 511, 516.

JOHANNES HOFINGER

Excerpts from *Worship: The Life of the Missions,* Johnannes Hofinger. Copyright © 1958, University of Notre Dame Press. Used with permission.

WE CANNOT LIVE WITHOUT THE MASS: *Worship: The Life of the Missions,* 8–9.

LITURGICAL FORMATION FOR MISSION: *Worship: The Life of the Missions,* 14.

CHRISTIAN LIVING IS MANIFEST AT THE LITURGY: *Worship: The Life of the Missions,* 14, 27–28.

CONTEMPLATION: *Worship: The Life of the Missions,* 277.

PARTICIPATION FROM WITHIN: *Worship: The Life of the Missions,* 280.

CLIFFORD HOWELL

BODY OF CHRIST: *Of Sacraments and Sacrifice,* (Collegeville: The Liturgical Press, 1952), 31–32. Used with permission.

CHISTIAN JOY: *Of Sacraments and Sacrifice,* (Collegeville: The Liturgical Press, 1952), 174–75. Used with permission.

WILLIAM HUELSMANN

SOLIDARITY: "Life in Christ," *Orate Fratres* 11 (1937): 257–58.

TO THE FATHER: "Parish Worship," *National Liturgical Week,* 1940, 126.

OUR COMMUNION WITH ONE ANOTHER: "Life in Christ," *Orate Fratres* 11 (1937): 473.

JOSEF A. JUNGMANN

HANDING ON THE FAITH: "Pastoral Effect," *Orate Fratres* 23 (1949): 491.

OUR OFFERING IS ONE WITH CHRIST: "We Offer," *Orate Fratres* 24 (1950): 101.

LITURGY AND HOLINESS: "We Offer," *Orate Fratres* 25 (1950): 102.

ASSEMBLY THROUGH BAPTISM AND EUCHARIST: "Holy Church," *Worship* 30 (1955): 7–8.

LITURGY ITSELF FORMS CHRISTIANS: "The Pastoral Idea," *Worship* 30 (1956): 615–16.

SHAPING ALL OUR PRAYER: "The Pastoral Idea," *Worship* 30 (1956): 619.

THE IMPORTANCE OF HISTORY: From *The Early Liturgy*, Josef A. Jungmann, 2, 4–5. Copyright © 1959, University of Notre Dame Press. Used with permission.

LITURGICAL SOURCES: From *The Early Liturgy*, Josef A. Jungmann, 5–7. Copyright © 1959, University of Notre Dame Press. Used with permission.

MYSTAGOGY: Josef A. Jungmann, *The Mass: An historical, theological and pastoral survey* (Collegeville: The Liturgical Press, 1976), 262–63. Used with permission.

PROPER CELEBRATION: Josef A. Jungmann, *The Mass: An historical, theological and pastoral survey* (Collegeville: The Liturgical Press, 1976), 263. Used with permission.

JAMES KLEIST

LITURGICAL ADAPTATION: "An Early Christian Prayer," *Orate Fratres* 22 (1948): 201.

EUCHARIST AND MARTYRDOM: "An Early Christian Prayer," *Orate Fratres* 22 (1948): 206.

BERNARD LAUKEMPER

THE PARISH DOES THE LITURGY: "To the Editor," *Orate Fratres* 12 (1938): 378–79.

CLOSING THE GAP BETWEEN PRIEST AND PEWS: "Points in Practice," *Orate Fratres* 12 (1938): 512.

MAURICE LAVANOUX

ENVIRONMENT AND ART: "Liturgical Art," *National Liturgical Week*, 1944, 75, 78–79.

THE AUTHENTIC TRADITION IN ART: "The Authentic Tradition in Art," *Liturgical Arts* 22:4 (New York: Liturgical Arts Society, 1954), 122–24.

WILLIAM LEONARD

PARTICIPATION IN LITURGY: *America* 109:25 (New York: America, 1963), 147–48. Used with permission.

LITURGY AND LIFE: *New Horizons in Catholic Worship* (Wichita, Kansas: The Liturgical Commission, 1964), 62.

FREDERICK McMANUS

STANDING IS A SIGN OF JOY: "Responses," *Worship* 33 (1959): 602–3.

LITURGICAL LAW: "Law, Liturgy and Participation," *North American Liturgical Week*, 1959, 45–46.

NO IVORY TOWER: *North American Liturgical Week*, 1961, 6.

JOHN XXIII AND THE COMING COUNCIL: *North American Liturgical Week*, 1961, 4.

THE RESPONSIBILITY: *North American Liturgical Week*, 1962, 107–8.

COLUMBA MARMION

PSALMS AND LITURGY: *Christ the Life of the Soul,* quoted in *Orate Fratres* 22 (1948): 547.

MICHAEL MATHIS

LITURGY IS AN ART: Selection from Robert J. Kennedy, *Michael Mathis: American Liturgical Pioneer.* Copyright © 1987, The Pastoral Press, Washington D.C. Used with permission.

KEEPING VIGIL FOR SUNDAY: "The Vigil Service," *North American Liturgical Week,* 1957, 186.

THOMAS MERTON

AT PEACE WITH TIME: Excerpt from *Seasons of Celebration,* Thomas Merton. Copyright © 1965, Abbey of Gethsemani. Reprinted by permission of Farrar, Strauss and Giroux, Inc., New York.

THE PSALMS ARE POETRY: From *Bread in the Wilderness,* Thomas Merton. Copyright © 1953, Our Lady of Gethsemani Monastery. Reprinted by permission of the Merton Legacy Trust.

ASHES, A SIGN OF RESURRECTION: Excerpt from *Seasons of Celebration,* Thomas Merton. Copyright © 1965, Abbey of Gethsemani. Reprinted by permission of Farrar, Strauss and Giroux, Inc., New York.

EXPERIMENTATION AND PATIENCE: Excerpt from *Seeds of Destruction,* Thomas Merton. Copyright © 1961, 1962, 1963, 1964, Abbey of Gethsemani. Reprinted by permission of Farrar, Straus and Giroux, Inc., New York.

VIRGIL MICHEL

LITURGY AND RELIGIOUS EXPERIENCE: Paraphrased and quoted by Paul Marx in *Virgil Michel and the Liturgical Movement* (Collegeville: The Liturgical Press, 1957), 222. Used with permission.

LITURGY DEMANDS PARTICIPATION: From *The Liturgy of the Church,* Virgil Michel. Copyright 1937, The Macmillan Company; copyright renewed © 1965, The Order of St. Benedict. Reprinted by permission of Macmillan Publishing Company, New York.

WORSHIP AND PRIVATE DEVOTIONS: Paul Marx, *Virgil Michel and the Liturgical Movement* (Collegeville: The Liturgical Press, 1957), 63. Used with permission.

LEARNING TO DO THE LITURGY: "Modern Greed and the Mass," *Orate Fratres* 11 (1937): 323–24.

LITURGY, THE BASIS: Virgil Michel quoted in *Orate Fratres* 15 (1941): 367.

JOSEPHINE MORGAN

LITURGY AND MUSIC: Josephine Morgan, an unpublished manuscript, "Preparing the Teacher to Meet the Challenge," used as an address in St. Louis in the middle to late 1960s.

JOSEPH P. MORRISON

ALL ARE ONE IN CHRIST: "The Racial Problem," *National Liturgical Week,* 1943, 113–14.

LITURGY AND DAILY LIFE: "Using Sacramentals," *Orate Fratres* 24 (1950): 132.

THERESE MUELLER

DOMESTIC CHURCH: "The Christian Family and the Liturgy," *National Liturgical Week,* 1941, 163, 165.

FAMILY AND FORMATION IN FAITH: "Poor Buster Brown," *Orate Fratres* 21 (1947): 110–12.

JANE MARIE MURRAY

DEVOTION TO MARY: "Mary our Mother," *Orate Fratres* 11 (1937): 392.

LENT, AN ANNUAL RETREAT: "Lenten
Mortification," *Orate Fratres* 17
(1943): 194.

LENTEN MORTIFICATION: "Lenten Mortification," *Orate Fratres* 17 (1943):
195–96.

JOHN P. O'CONNELL

BAPTISM AND WORSHIP: "Grafted in the
Vine," *National Liturgical Week,* 1948,
47.

PRIESTHOOD AND SACRIFICE: "The
Priesthood of Christ," *National Liturgical Week,* 1951, 19, 25.

PIUS PARSCH

PRAYING WITH THE RITES: "The Apostolate," *Orate Fratres* 22 (1947): 46.

SEASONS AND PLAY: "How to Interpret
the Season," *Orate Fratres* 22 (1947): 1.

A BLESSING FOR THE HOMILY: "Sunday
Sermons," *Orate Fratres* 22 (1948): 108.

HANS ANSGAR REINHOLD

VESTMENTS: "More Or Less Liturgical,"
Orate Fratres 13 (1939): 153.

FRUIT OF THE EARTH: "More or Less
Liturgical," *Orate Fratres* 13 (1939):
154.

BECOMING LITURGICAL: "More or Less
Liturgical," *Orate Fratres* 13 (1939):
154–55.

GUESTS OR MEMBERS: "Christian
Transients—Transient Christians?"
Orate Fratres 13 (1939): 275–76.

LITURGY AND POPULAR DEVOTIONS:
"Parish Worship: Devotions," *National
Liturgical Week,* 1940, 170–75.

LAYING DOWN OUR LIVES: "Social
Leaven," *Orate Fratres* 25 (1951):
518–19.

WILD GROWTH IS CUT AWAY: *Bringing
the Mass to the People* (Baltimore:
Helicon Press, 1960), 102–3.

JOHN ROSS-DUGGAN

THE USE OF ENGLISH: From a manuscript, in a summary for the Vernacular
Society, 1950.

LEO RUDLOFF

LITURGY IS ALWAYS A PUBLIC ACT: *Every-
man's Theology,* Leo Rudloff, 122.
Copyright © 1942, Bruce Publishing
Company, Mission Hills, California.
Used with permission.

GIVING PRAISE AND THANKS: "Private
Prayer and the Liturgy," *National Liturgical Week,* 1945, 26–27.

MARY PERKINS RYAN

TRUE PIETY: *National Liturgical Week,*
1940, 153.

A PERSON INTERESTED: *The Sacramental
Way,* Mary Perkins Ryan, 38–39.
Copyright © 1948, Sheed and Ward,
Kansas City, Missouri. Used with
permission.

SHAWN SHEEHAN

Excerpts from *Liturgy for the People,*
ed. William Leonard. Copyright ©
1963, Bruce Publishing Company,
Mission Hills, California. Used with
permission.

IMPORTANCE OF REPARATION: *National
Liturgical Week,* 1945, 31.

PARTICIPATION: *Liturgy for the People,*
75.

ASH WEDNESDAY: *Liturgy for the People,* 80.

THE ACT OF ASSEMBLING: *Liturgy for
the People,* 84–85.

GERARD SLOYAN

THE BIBLE AND LITURGY: "Read the Bible, and . . . ," *Worship* 26 (1952): 150–51.

READING THE BIBLE: "Reading the Bible: Some Suggestions," *Worship* 26 (1952): 311–12.

RELEVANCE TO LIFE: *North American Liturgical Week,* 1962, 109–12.

JOSEPH F. STEDMAN

PARTICIPATION IN THE MASS: *My Sunday Missal,* Joseph F. Stedman, 12–13, 22–23. Copyright © 1938, Confraternity of the Precious Blood, New York. Used with permission.

BASIL STEGMAN

THE LIFE OF THE CHURCH: "Christian Life and Worship," *Orate Fratres* 7 (1933): 550.

THE PSALMS: "Liturgy and the Scriptures," *Orate Fratres* 10 (1936): 515–16.

GEORGIA STEVENS

CHANT WITH CHILDREN: *Gregorian Chant* (New York: The Macmillan Publishing Company, 1946), VI-84.

WHERE DID CHANT COME FROM: "Gregorian Chant, The Greatest Unison Music," *The Catholic Choirmaster* 30:3, 1944, 102. Originally published in *Musical Quarterly.*

ANSELM STOLZ

MYSTICISM IS: "Mysticism is the Natural Flowering of the Sacramental Life," *Orate Fratres* 17 (1943): 397.

SAMUEL STRITCH

AGAINST SPIRITUAL INDIVIDUALISM: *National Liturgical Week,* 1940, 2.

THE CORPORATE NATURE OF THE CHURCH: "Sermon," *National Liturgical Week,* 1940, 238.

KATHRYN SULLIVAN

LOVE OF THE PSALMS: "Scripture in Worship," *Worship* 29 (1955): 193.

MARY IN LITURGY: "Book of Esther," *Worship* 30 (1956): 451–52.

THE LORD BE WITH YOU: "The Book of Ruth," *Worship* 30 (1956): 369–70.

AVAILABILITY: "The Constitution and the Religious Life, *North American Liturgical Week,* 1964, 255–56.

COLUMBAN THUIS

THE LITURGICAL ACTION: *National Liturgical Week,* 1941, 28.

CHRIST, THE LITURGIST: *National Liturgical Week,* 1946, 13.

GERALD VANN

THE DOUBLE LIFE OF SYMBOLS: *The Paradise Tree,* Gerald Vann, 16–17. Copyright © 1959, Sheed & Ward, Kansas City, Missouri. Used with permission.

ERMIN VITRY

THE SACRAMENTALITY OF SACRED MUSIC: "Music and Prayer," *Orate Fratres* 25 (1951): 556.

CHRISTMAS: "To Know Him Whom We Already Know," *Worship* 28 (1954): 68–69.

ASCENSION: "Before the Throne," *Worship* 28 (1954): 279.

JUSTINE WARD

Excerpts from *Justine Ward and Solesmes*, Pierre Combe, published by The Catholic University of America Press, Washington, D.C. Copyright © 1987, Dom Mocquereau Foundation, New York. Used with permission.

THE APOSTOLATE OF CHURCH MUSIC: *Justine Ward and Solesmes*, 1.

WINGED WORDS OF ETERNAL LIFE: "Winged Words," *Orate Fratres* 1 (1927): 111–12.

SUNG PRAYER: *Justine Ward and Solesmes*, 132.

BEAUTY: *Justine Ward and Solesmes*, 90–91.

GREGORIAN CHANT: *Justine Ward and Solesmes*, 133.

ALOYSIUS WILMES

SINGING AT COMMUNION: "We Are Active at Mass," *National Liturgical Week*, 1947, 109.

REFORM OF THE EASTER VIGIL: "Active Participation in the New Rites and the Old," *National Liturgical Week*, 1952, 53–54.

MARY FABYAN WINDEATT

WE RECEIVE EACH OTHER: "Whom Shall We Love," *Orate Fratres* 16 (1942): 209–10.

THE SECRET OF COMMUNAL PRAYER: "Whom Shall We Love," *Orate Fratres* 16 (1942): 212.

DAMASUS WINZEN

CHRYSOSTOM ON THE WORK OF THE LAITY: "Parish Worship: The Mass," *National Liturgical Week*, 1940, 111–12.

LITURGICAL PREACHING: "The Liturgy and the Word of God," *National Liturgical Week*, 1944, 129–30.

JOHN D. WRIGHT

GOD'S CHOICE OF SINNERS: *National Liturgical Week*, 1949, 135.

SPERABAMUS: A MEDITATION ON EMMAUS: *North American Liturgical Week*, 1961, 2–3.

NOTES ON ILLUSTRATIONS

Art from *Orate Fratres* and *Worship* published by The Liturgical Press, Collegeville, Minnesota, is used with permission.

Liturgical Arts (New York: Liturgical Arts Society) and the *Catholic Art Quarterly* (Catholic Art Association) are out of print. It was not possible to trace the artists or copyright holders. We will be happy in future editions to include proper and specific acknowledgments. Artist's names, when known, appear in parentheses.

PAGE 14: *Orate Fratres* 6, no. 1 (1931): cover.

PAGE 20: *Liturgical Arts* 1, no. 3 (1932): 121. (Eric Gill)

PAGE 23: *The Catholic Art Quarterly* 10, no. 2 (1947): 40.

PAGE 29: *Liturgical Arts* 26, no. 1 (1957): 30.

PAGE 32: *Eye Contact with God through Pictures,* #9.4, Copyright © 1986, Ade Bethune. Published by Sheed and Ward, Kansas City, Missouri. Used with permission.

PAGE 38: *Orate Fratres* 2, no. 6 (1928): 171.

PAGE 44: *Orate Fratres* 1, no. 1 (1926): 25.

PAGE 49: *Liturgical Arts* 17, no. 4 (1948): 131.

PAGE 53: *Orate Fratres* 6, no. 11 (1930): 505.

PAGE 57: *Orate Fratres* 3, no. 7 (1929): cover.

PAGE 60: *Orate Fratres* 3, no. 2 (1928): 49.

PAGE 64: *Orate Fratres* 6, no. 6 (1932): 254.

PAGE 66: *The Catholic Art Quarterly* 10, no. 1 (1946): 25. (Phillip Hagreen)

PAGE 69: *Liturgical Arts* 26, no. 1 (1957): 29. (Frank Kacmarcik)

PAGE 72: *Saint Andrew Daily Missal,* Dom Gaspar Lefebvre. St. Paul, Minnesota: The E. M. Lohmann Co., 1949, 1953; 459.

PAGE 75: *Liturgical Arts* 1, no. 4 (1932): 145. (Eric Gill)

PAGE 78: *The Catholic Art Quarterly* 10, no. 2 (1947): 41. (Jesse Buckles)

PAGE 83: *The Catholic Art Quarterly* 8, no. 1 (1944): 16.

PAGE 86: *The Catholic Art Quarterly* 6, no. 1 (1942): 30. (Sister Joan [of the Medical Mission Sisters])

PAGE 90: *Orate Fratres* 3, no. 2 (1928): cover.

PAGE 100: *Orate Fratres* 10, no. 1 (1935): 53.

PAGE 103: *Orate Fratres* 1, no. 8 (1927): 230.

PAGE 106: *Orate Fratres* 9, no. 9 (1935): 416.

PAGE 109: *The Catholic Art Quarterly* 10, no. 2 (1947): 41. (Frank Kacmarcik)

PAGE 113: *Liturgical Arts* 13, no. 4 (1945): 90. (Paul Bornet)

PAGE 120: *Saint Andrew Daily Missal,* Dom Gaspar Lefebvre. St. Paul, Minnesota: The E. M. Lohmann Company, 1949, 1953; 349.

PAGE 124: *Saint Andrew Daily Missal,* Dom Gaspar Lefebvre. St. Paul, Minnesota: The E. M. Lohmann Company, 1949, 1953; 147.

PAGE 128: *The Catholic Art Quarterly* 6, no. 1 (1942): 6. (Mary Katherine Finnegan)

PAGE 131: *The Catholic Art Quarterly* 6, no. 1 (1942): 27. (Mary Katherine Finnegan)

PAGE 136: *Orate Fratres* 1, no. 4 (1927): 102.

PAGE 138: *Orate Fratres* 13, no. 3 (1939): 101.

PAGE 143: *Orate Fratres* 3, no. 4 (1929): cover.

PAGE 146: *Liturgical Arts* 24, no. 2 (1956): 27.

PAGE 149: *Orate Fratres* 13, no. 11 (1939): 515.

PAGE 151: *The Catholic Art Quarterly* 10, no. 1 (1946): 3.

PAGE 160: *The Catholic Art Quarterly* 7, no. 4 (1944): 11.

PAGE 163: *Liturgical Arts* 26, no. 1 (1957): 30. (Frank Kacmarcik)

PAGE 166: *The Catholic Art Quarterly* 10, no. 2 (1947): 41. (Ade Bethune)

PAGE 169: *The Catholic Art Quarterly* 10, no. 2 (1947): 33.

PAGE 172: *Orate Fratres* 6, no. 9 (1932): 409.

PAGE 177: *The Catholic Art Quarterly* 7, no. 2 (1944): 6.

PAGE 179: *The Catholic Art Quarterly* 10, no. 4 (1947): 105.

PAGE 181: *Orate Fratres* 7, no. 11 (1933): 495.

PAGE 186: *Orate Fratres* 14, no. 2 (1939): 78.

PAGE 190: *Orate Fratres* 15, no. 11 (1940): cover.

PAGE 192: *The Catholic Art Quarterly* 6, no. 1 (1942): 30. (Sister Joan)

PAGE 195: *Orate Fratres* 6, no. 7 (1932): cover.

PAGE 198: *Orate Fratres* 9, no. 4 (1935): 166.

PAGE 201: *Eye Contact with God through Pictures, #9.3,* Copyright © 1986, Ade Bethune. Published by Sheed and Ward, Kansas City, Missouri. Used with permission.

PAGE 203: *The Catholic Art Quarterly* 10, no. 1 (1946): 17.

PAGE 206: *The Catholic Art Quarterly* 10, no. 1 (1946): 1.

PAGE 214: *National Liturgical Week,* 1950, 62.

PAGE 217: *Orate Fratres* 13, no. 6 (1939): 247.

PAGE 219: *Liturgical Arts* 15, no. 2 (1946): 56.

PAGE 221: *Orate Fratres* 1, no. 2 (1926): 58.

PAGE 225: *The Catholic Art Quarterly* 10, no. 1 (1946): 24.

PAGE 231: *The Catholic Art Quarterly* 10, no. 1 (1946): 3.

PAGE 234: *The Catholic Art Quarterly* 10, no. 1 (1946): 17.

PAGE 236: *Orate Fratres* 14, no. 8 (1940): 352.

PAGE 239: *Orate Fratres* 13, no. 9 (1939): 405.

PAGE 241: *The Catholic Art Quarterly* 6, no. 1 (1942): 30. (Sister Joan)

PAGE 243: *Orate Fratres* 9, no. 2
(1934): 80.

PAGE 247: *Orate Fratres* 6, no. 5
(1932): 218.

PAGE 249: *Orate Fratres* 13, no. 6
(1939): cover.

PAGE 251: *Orate Fratres* 15, no. 9
(1941): 416.

PAGE 254: *Orate Fratres* 7, no. 3
(1933): 107.

PAGE 257: *Liturgical Arts* 21, no. 2
(1953): 35. (Phillip Hagreen)

PAGE 259: *Orate Fratres* 6, no. 12
(1932): 525.

PAGE 261: *Orate Fratres* 15, no. 6
(1941): cover.

PAGE 265: *The Catholic Art Quarterly*
10, no. 2 (1947): 41. (Ade Bethune)

INDEX

Active participation, 76, 88, 92, 97, 121, 135, 142, 147, 170, 187, 202, 215, 223, 232
Apostolate, liturgical. *See* Movement, liturgical
Architecture, church, 125, 129, 167
Art, 36, 125, 135, 167, 168, 207
Availability, 246

Baptism, 73, 96, 110, 202

Catechesis, 40, 152, 159, 235
  of children, 73, 74, 197
Chant, 237, 255, 256
Christ, 15, 16, 27, 152, 248
Chrysostom, 262
Church, 25, 51, 52, 101, 121, 153
  corporate nature of, 107, 242, 260
  domestic, 30, 31, 196, 197
Communion, 147, 258, 260
Confirmation, 41
Contemplation, 141

Divine Office. *See* Liturgy of the Hours

Eucharist, 51, 94, 101, 110, 161, 218, 267. *See also* Mass
  blessed sacrament, reservation of, 28

Food, 33, 207

Greeting, 245
Gueranger, 27

Homily, 76, 129, 158, 205, 263
  (includes liturgical preaching)

Individualism, 54, 134, 242

Laity, 22, 30, 31, 97, 262
Language, inclusive, 150
Law, liturgical, 91, 173
Liturgical prayer, 129, 154, 204, 209, 218
  beauty of, 24
  communal nature of, 17, 25, 121, 134, 188, 224, 258, 260
  sung, 256
Liturgy
  formative power of, 140, 153
  history of, 155, 157
  meaning of, 135, 145, 152, 153, 169, 187, 207
  nature of, 24, 25, 26, 47, 56, 70, 87, 88, 105, 118
  purpose of, 118
Liturgy and life, 50, 54, 62, 84, 102, 129, 130, 133, 134, 140, 153, 170, 174, 180, 188, 208, 211, 220, 235
Liturgy and time, 182
Liturgy of the Hours, 80, 180, 244, 256

Mary, 199, 244
Mass, 51, 82, 94, 101, 111, 139, 147.
  See also eucharist
Movement, liturgical, 27, 45, 55, 67, 68, 95
Music, 191, 237, 252, 256, 258.
  See Chant
Mystical Body, 17, 107, 110, 125, 135, 144, 147, 165, 193, 248
Mysticism, 240

Parish, 95, 125, 127, 164, 165, 208
Piety, 107, 220, 222
Posture, 37, 115, 116, 173
Praise, 132, 164, 218
Preaching. *See* homily
Priesthood, 202
Psalms, 178, 183, 235, 244

Reform, American context of, 122
  dangers in, 98
  how to implement, 95, 122, 125, 132, 137
  necessity of, 40, 43, 45, 121, 161, 175, 185, 212
Reparation, 222

Sacraments, 15, 16, 24, 110, 240
Saints, 33
Scripture, 39, 43, 47, 50, 58, 92, 178, 183, 226, 227, 235, 245. *See* psalms
Social concern, 62, 84, 133, 189
Sunday, 21, 61, 62, 180
Symbols, 36, 58, 70, 114, 115, 184, 207, 250

Vernacular, 39, 65, 215
Vestments, 207

Word of God. *See* scripture

Year, liturgical, 30, 45, 71, 81, 104, 108, 127, 199, 200, 205, 223, 252, 253, 258
  (includes seasons and feasts except Sunday)